PRIMROSE BAKERY
CHRISTMAS

For my dad, Jeremy

Published by Square Peg 2014

9 8 7 6 5 4 3 2

Copyright © Martha Swift 2014
Photography by Stuart Ovenden © Square Peg 2014

Martha Swift has asserted her rights under the Copyright, Designs
and Patents Act 1988 to be identified as the author of this work

First published in Great Britain in 2014 by
Square Peg
20 Vauxhall Bridge Road,
London SW1V 2SA

A Penguin Random House company

www.vintage-books.co.uk
www.penguinrandomhouse.com

A CIP catalogue record for this book
is available from the British Library

ISBN 9780224098953

Photography: Stuart Ovenden
Illustrations: Michael Heath
Design: Friederike Huber
Styling: Martha Swift and Alice Whiting
Food styling: Lisa Chan and Daniel Harding

Penguin Random House supports the Forest Stewardship
Council® (FSC®), the leading international forest-certification
organisation. Our books carrying the FSC label are printed on
FSC®-certified paper. FSC is the only forest-certification scheme
supported by the leading environmental organisations, including
Greenpeace. Our paper procurement policy can be found at
www.randomhouse.co.uk/environment

Printed and bound in China by C&C Offset Printing Co., Ltd

PRIMROSE BAKERY CHRISTMAS

Martha Swift

◧ SQUARE PEG

CONTENTS

SWEET! SWEET!

INTRODUCTION

The idea for a Christmas book came about through a desire to combine the traditional ideas of Christmas baking with the Primrose Bakery idea of Christmas. Christmas is probably the biggest celebration of the year for many people round the world, and in my two shops we all have a lot of fun with Christmas cupcakes, cakes, decorations, presents and a general feeling of happiness – more than probably at any other time of year. For me on a personal level, it is the one time of year I let my mum come and work in the shop, which she looks forward to all year round, although it is often hard to get her to stop chatting to everyone and actually work!

At Christmas we look forward to the end of the year, usually to have some time off work, a chance to catch up with family and friends, to eat and drink more than usual and hopefully to get a chance to relax and enjoy this special time. There is often more time to do some baking, either for yourself and your family or to make delicious gifts and treats to take to parties and get-togethers or simply give as Christmas presents. The recipes in this book do not only have to be made at Christmas and are not all Christmas-specific, more a collection of some of our recipes that we think work particularly well at this time of year and ones that can be given as gifts or used as decorations. Many of them you will find in our shops both in December and popping up through the year. Hopefully it is also a book you will come back to at many times through the year to find a favourite recipe, or indeed a book that could itself be given as a present.

This is the bakery's fourth book and also marks ten years since Primrose Bakery was founded. I can't believe that ten years have gone by already – although I am secretly happy, as I was recently told that it is only once your business has been running for ten years that you can consider it established and a success. I am so glad I didn't know that three years in! In the time since Lisa and I wrote *Celebrations* there have been some big changes at the bakery, which I hope have not been too noticeable to our customers but which I think are vital for the continued success of the bakery. In November 2013 Lisa decided to pursue other interests she had away from Primrose Bakery and we decided I would take over as sole owner – I am so happy that we founded the business together ten years ago and will miss her huge creative input and presence – but I am also excited to take the bakery into the next ten years and beyond. Primrose Bakery never was and never will be just about the two of us: we are backed by all the amazing and talented staff we employ, both in the kitchens and in the shops, and all our books are a reflection of this team effort. In the last ten years we have developed more than 70 flavours of cupcake, although chocolate and vanilla remain the most popular, closely followed by salted caramel. You will find some of our latest flavours here, which I hope still remain simple to prepare.

Even ten years on, the bakery kitchens remain a combination of home and professional. There is still no huge equipment and we still bake in small batches. We source the best ingredients we can and try to stick to using seasonal produce. I truly believe this helps us maintain the high quality of our cupcakes and cakes, and I also believe it helps keep the recipes in the books simple to follow and delicious. The development of new recipes remains a group effort, and for this book I have tried to encourage every member of my staff to get involved – especially to keep in with the Christmas idea of bringing everyone together. The days and hours working at the bakery can be long and sometimes stressful, and it is a credit to the chefs who work there that they are always cheerful and passionate about their baking. For this book I must give special credit to our former head chef, Lisa Chan, who sadly had to leave the UK in October 2013 to return home to Australia but who has been a vital part of this book and who I hope will be involved in the bakery for many years to come, wherever she may be living.

I have been lucky enough to travel to some amazing countries in the last few years and wherever I go I try to find the local cake shops, cake decorations and baking equipment. One of my favourite things to do is to find the local supermarkets and markets and discover new ingredients and flavours that might find their way back to our kitchens to be incorporated into a new cupcake or cake recipe. I have been to Singapore a few times and, apart from the beautiful weather, find the people there passionate about food and anything new – the cupcakes craze has really taken off there in recent years. I am hoping to open a Primrose Bakery some-where in Asia in the next few years. At the same time, I have also been inspired by some of the ingredients and favourite tastes I have tried in many different countries and, given the many different nationalities I employ, to try to include recipes in this book that include Christmas baking from different parts of the world.

Christmas for me will always, however, remain a quintessentially English time of year, with a Christmas tree, stockings, turkey, carols and mountains of wrapping paper to recycle. My two daughters are now sixteen and nineteen but still expect Father Christmas to visit on Christmas Eve and for us all to eat too much chocolate on Christmas Day. In the last year, my eldest daughter, Daisy, has started working at Primrose Bakery part-time while she is studying at university. It has been a huge pleasure to have her working there and has meant it continues to be a real family business – and I am hoping that her sister Millie will soon join her and work a few days a week. I am also hoping to open another Primrose Bakery or two in the very near future, but will always try to maintain the small business feel and quality that we started out with ten years ago.

CUPCAKES

Primrose Bakery started making cupcakes some ten years ago, and we are still not tired of them! As ever, they fit all occasions – Christmas is no different, and the cupcakes you will find in this chapter should work well at this festive time. There are some slightly more adventurous flavours here, but the recipes are still straightforward and easy to follow and the results are just as delicious.

Working on new cupcake flavours is one of the best parts of owning and working at the bakery. We have tried to stay imaginative and a bit quirky without becoming carried away dreaming up flavours that are too ridiculous. For whatever reason, cupcakes lend themselves very well to a whole range of flavour combinations, while managing also to look very pretty and tempting. They also make a great gift or celebration food.

Wherever possible, use free-range or organic eggs and the highest-quality vanilla extract you can afford. These small things will make a subtle but noticeable difference to your finished cupcakes. Please note that cupcakes brown very quickly when cooking and will still feel soft, but they will become very hard if overcooked.

TEA AND DIGESTIVES CUPCAKES

Probably the most English of customs, a cup of tea and a digestive biscuit mark the end of many people's day, or a mid-morning break. We decided to combine the two into a cupcake, and what could be nicer than one of these after a long and tiring day of Christmas shopping?

Makes 17 regular cupcakes

CUPCAKES

200ml milk
6 English Breakfast tea bags
220g unsalted butter, at room temperature
270g granulated sugar
3 large eggs
240g self-raising flour
a pinch of salt
17 digestive biscuits, plus extra, crushed,
  to decorate

Preheat the oven to 180°C/160°C (fan)/ gas mark 4. Line two 12-hole muffin tins with 17 muffin cases.

Bring the milk to the boil on the hob or in the microwave. Add the tea bags and cover with cling film. Set aside to steep for at least 30 minutes. When ready to use, squeeze out the excess liquid from the tea bags. Throw the tea bags away and keep the milk to one side.

Cream the butter and sugar together in a bowl with an electric hand mixer until light and fluffy. Add the eggs one at a time, ensuring each is well combined before adding the next.

Add half the flour and the salt and mix until just combined. Pour half the tea-infused milk into the mixture and beat again. Add the remaining flour and milk in turn until it is all combined.

Break 6 digestive biscuits into 3 pieces each and place one piece in the bottom of each muffin case. Spoon the cupcake batter over each biscuit piece, filling the case to about two-thirds full.

Break the remaining whole digestives into 4 or

5 pieces. Insert 2 or 3 pieces into each case of cupcake batter, on an angle. Do not place them flat on top of the batter, as this will prevent the batter from rising.

Bake the cupcakes for 18–20 minutes, or until an inserted skewer comes out clean. Allow the cupcakes to cool in their trays for about 10 minutes, then place on a wire rack to cool completely.

MILKY TEA BUTTERCREAM

100ml milk
4 English Breakfast tea bags
150g unsalted butter, at room temperature
550g icing sugar, sifted

Pour the milk into a pan and bring to the boil on the hob or in the microwave. Add the tea bags and cover with cling film. Set aside to steep until completely cooled. When cooled, squeeze out the excess liquid from the tea bags. Throw the tea bags away.

Put the butter, icing sugar and tea-infused milk into a large bowl and mix using the low speed of an electric mixer until all the ingredients are combined. Scrape down the sides, then mix the icing again on a medium to high speed for about a minute, until the icing is light and fluffy.

ASSEMBLE

Ice the cupcakes with the buttercream and top with roughly crushed digestive biscuits.

CRUNCHIE CUPCAKES

One of our newer range of chocolate-bar themed cupcakes, these honey-flavoured sponges topped with milk chocolate icing and a piece of Crunchie bar make a sweet treat on a cold Christmas afternoon and would go down well with a huge range of ages, I am sure!

Makes 10 regular cupcakes

CUPCAKES

110g unsalted butter, at room temperature
130g clear, liquid honey
1 large egg
50ml vegetable oil
50g soft brown sugar
170g plain flour
¾ teaspoon bicarbonate of soda
a pinch of salt
extra honey, for brushing

Preheat the oven to 180°C/160°C (fan)/gas mark 4. Line a 12-hole muffin tin with 10 muffin cases.

Put the butter and honey into a microwaveable bowl. Heat in a microwave very carefully in short bursts (probably up to a maximum of 30 seconds), until the butter has melted. Stir to combine.

Add the egg and mix with an electric hand mixer until thoroughly combined. Add the oil and sugar and beat together. Add the flour, bicarbonate of soda and salt, and mix again until the batter is smooth.

Spoon the mixture evenly into the muffin cases. Bake in the oven for approximately 20 minutes, until an inserted skewer comes out clean. Please note that the cupcakes brown very quickly when cooking and will still feel soft, but they will become very hard if they are overcooked.

Once the cupcakes are out of the oven, brush each one generously with honey and set aside to cool completely.

MILK CHOCOLATE ICING

**300g good-quality milk chocolate, broken
into small pieces**
4 tablespoons double cream
30g unsalted butter
½ teaspoon vanilla extract

Melt the chocolate either in a heatproof bowl
over a pan of simmering water on the hob (the
bowl should not touch the water) or carefully
in a suitable bowl in the microwave. Once it has
melted and cooled very briefly, add the cream,
butter and vanilla and beat well until smooth
and combined. It will probably need to go into
the fridge for about 30 minutes to set a little
before using. You may need to beat it once again
before icing.

ASSEMBLE

**2–3 Crunchie bars, cut into 3 pieces each,
to decorate**

Ice the cupcakes with the milk chocolate icing
and top each one with a piece of cut-up
Crunchie bar.
  Any unused icing should be stored in the fridge.

MALTESER CUPCAKES

The first confectionery-themed cupcake we developed, this really is now a firm favourite for many, even catching up with salted caramel cupcakes. The only question is – how many Maltesers should you decorate each one with?

Makes 18 regular cupcakes

CUPCAKES

200g unsalted butter, at room temperature
150g golden caster sugar
60g soft brown sugar
½ teaspoon vanilla extract
3 large eggs
250g self-raising flour
150g Ovaltine
¼ teaspoon salt
100ml milk
70g crushed Maltesers

Preheat the oven to 180°C/160°C (fan)/ gas mark 4. Line two 12-hole muffin tins with 18 muffin cases.

Using an electric hand mixer, cream the butter, sugars and vanilla until the mixture is light and fluffy. Add the eggs one at a time, ensuring that each is well combined before adding the next.

Add half the flour, Ovaltine and salt, then half of the milk, beating after each addition until the mixture is just combined. Repeat this step with the remaining flour, ovaltine, salt and milk.

Fold in the crushed Maltesers, using a rubber spatula. Set aside to rest for 10 minutes.

Fold the mixture again until it is smooth and only a few air bubbles remain. Spoon the mixture evenly into the muffin cases.

Bake for 18–20 minutes. Do not place the tins on the bottom rack of the oven – the middle one is much better. The cupcakes will be ready when an inserted skewer comes out clean, even though they may still seem quite soft and not firm to the touch. If you overcook them they will harden quickly.

Leave to cool in their tins for about 10 minutes, and then place on a wire rack to cool completely.

MALTESER BUTTERCREAM ICING

120g milk chocolate
70g dark chocolate (70% cocoa solids)
200g unsalted butter, at room temperature
50g Ovaltine
400g icing sugar
50ml milk

Melt the milk and dark chocolate very carefully in a suitable bowl in the microwave or in a heatproof bowl over a pan of simmering water on the hob. Set aside to cool slightly.

Put the butter, Ovaltine, icing sugar and milk into a bowl. Using a electric mixer, beat on a low speed until it is well combined. Scrape down the sides of the bowl. Increase the speed to medium/high for 30 seconds, then scrape down again.

Pour in the melted chocolate and beat again on a low speed until everything is thoroughly combined.

ASSEMBLE

Maltesers, to decorate

Ice the cupcakes with the Malteser icing and decorate with as many Maltesers as you would like!

✴ PRIMROSE BAKERY FLAVOURS ✴
➔ DAILY ➔

Carrot
Chocolate
Chocolate & Vanilla
Gluten Free
Red Velvet
Salted Caramel
Vanilla

★ DAILY SPECIALS ★

Monday: Cookies & Cream, Rose
Tuesday: Choc Caramel, Maple Pecan
Wednesday: Lemon, Toblerone
Thursday: Choc Banana
            Choc Marshmallow
            Malteser
Friday: Cinnamon, Cocktail Flavour,
         Mocha, Peanut Butter

Saturday: Apple Crumble, Crunchie,
           Malteser, Rose

Sunday: Banoffee, Choc White Choc,
         Earl Grey, Toblerone

TOBLERONE CUPCAKES

Another favourite chocolate at Christmas time, these cupcakes really capture the taste of chewy honey and almond nougat Toblerone and won't last long on any table.

Makes 16 regular cupcakes

CUPCAKES

150g self-raising flour
100g cocoa powder
220g unsalted butter, at room temperature
250g soft brown sugar
3 large eggs
1 teaspoon vanilla extract
120ml milk
3 x 100g bars of Toblerone, cut into
  individual segments

Preheat the oven to 180°C/160°C (fan)/gas mark 4. Line two 12-hole muffin tins with 16 muffin cases.

Sift the flour and cocoa powder into a bowl and set aside.

Cream the butter and sugar together in another bowl with an electric mixer for 3–5 minutes, or until light and fluffy. Add the eggs one at a time, ensuring each one is thoroughly combined before you add the next.

Add the vanilla and beat again. Add the flour and cocoa powder and mix until just combined. Pour in the milk and beat until the batter is smooth.

Spoon the mixture evenly into the muffin cases. Place a piece of Toblerone in each one.

Bake for 15–18 minutes, or until an inserted skewer comes out clean. Leave to cool in their tins for about 10 minutes, then place on a wire rack to cool completely.

CHOCOLATE HONEY ICING

100g milk chocolate
100g unsalted butter, at room temperature
30g clear liquid honey
50ml milk
500g icing sugar

Put the chocolate into a suitable bowl and melt
very carefully in a microwave, or melt in a
heatproof bowl on top of a pan of simmering
water on the hob. Set aside to cool slightly.

Put the butter, honey and milk into another
bowl and beat well until combined. Sift in the
icing sugar and beat until the mixture is smooth.
Pour in the melted chocolate and beat again until
everything is thoroughly combined and you have
a smooth buttercream icing.

ASSEMBLE

Ice the cupcakes with the chocolate icing
and decorate with one piece of Toblerone
per cupcake.

PINK LEMONADE CUPCAKES

Developed by our former chef Laura Rogers, these pretty pink cupcakes remind us of summer and warmth while providing some much-needed colour for the Christmas table. This is a slightly harder cupcake to perfect, but follow the instructions very closely and it will be well worth the effort.

Makes 15 regular cupcakes

PINK LEMONADE SYRUP

225g granulated sugar
250ml water
juice of 2½ lemons
130g frozen or fresh raspberries

Start by making the pink lemonade syrup. Put the sugar and water in a pan and bring to the boil, stirring to make sure all the sugar dissolves. Add the lemon juice and raspberries and turn off the heat.

Pour the mixture into a food processor and process until it becomes a smooth liquid. Strain the liquid through a fine sieve into a bowl to remove the raspberry seeds. Set aside to cool.

CUPCAKES

180g plain flour
2 teaspoons baking powder
4 large eggs
160g caster sugar
100g unsalted butter, melted
40ml corn oil
4 tablespoons pink lemonade syrup
4 tablespoons grenadine syrup
zest of 2 lemons

Preheat the oven to 180°C/160°C (fan)/gas mark 4. Line two 12-hole muffin tins with 15 muffin cases.

To make the cupcakes, sift the flour and baking powder into a bowl and set aside.

In another bowl whisk the eggs and sugar together with an electric mixer until the mixture is pale and fluffy and forms ribbons when you lift the beaters. Add the remaining wet ingredients and the lemon zest and beat gently.

Using a spatula, gently fold in one-third of the flour and baking powder. Then add the remaining flour and baking powder and fold again. Be careful not to knock too much air out of this batter. It will have a very liquid consistency.

Spoon into the muffin cases and bake immediately. It is really important not to allow this batter to sit and rest for too long, otherwise the cupcakes will be very flat. Bake for 12–15 minutes, or until golden brown and an inserted skewer comes out clean.

Leave to cool for 3–5 minutes, then prick each cupcake with a fork, to make some holes in the surface, and brush each one with some of the remaining pink lemonade syrup. The cakes must be brushed while they are still quite warm, so that they soak up the syrup more easily.

PINK LEMONADE ICING

For the sherbet
3 tablespoons citric acid
1 tablespoon bicarbonate of soda
12 tablespoons icing sugar

For the icing
150g sherbet (see above)
500g icing sugar
150g butter
130ml pink lemonade

Ideally, this icing should be made the night before you use it, so that it has time for the bicarbonate of soda to settle. If it is made on the day of icing, leave it for at least 4–5 hours to settle.

Sift the sherbet ingredients together into a bowl and set aside.

Place all the other icing ingredients in a bowl and mix together using an electric mixer, until the mixture becomes smooth and lump-free. Add the sherbet and beat again.

ASSEMBLE

pink glitter or sprinkles, to decorate

Before using this icing, beat it vigorously to remove all the air bubbles so that it is smooth.

Ice the cupcakes with the pink lemonade icing and decorate with some pink sugar decorations and/or glitter.

LIQUORICE ALLSORTS CUPCAKES

These really are love them or hate them cupcakes, as Liquorice Allsorts are an acquired taste and you can either not get enough of them or never want to touch them. We launched these at the London Cake and Bake show in September 2013, and they would look so festive on a tier with all the different colours decorating each one.

Makes 14 regular cupcakes

STAR ANISE MILK
(for use in cupcakes and icing)

3 medium whole star anise
130ml milk

Place the star anise in the milk and heat carefully in the microwave or in a pan on the hob until it boils. Wrap the bowl in cling film and set aside to cool.

LIQUORICE CUPCAKES

200g unsalted butter, at room temperature
225g golden caster sugar
2 large eggs
½ teaspoon vanilla extract
210g plain flour
1 teaspoon baking powder
a pinch of salt
75ml star anise milk (see method above)
120g Liquorice Allsorts roughly chopped
  into small pieces about 5mm in size

Preheat the oven to 180°C/160°C (fan)/gas mark 4. Line two 12-hole muffin tins with 14 muffin cases.

  Cream the butter and sugar together in a bowl until light and fluffy. Using an electric mixer, beat the eggs in one at a time on a medium speed, beating well after each addition. Add the vanilla with the last egg.

Sift the flour, baking powder and salt on to the top of the mixture. Beat on a low speed until it is just combined. Strain the star anise milk to remove the star anise and then pour into the batter and mix until smooth. Fold in the chopped Liquorice Allsorts with a spatula or wooden spoon.

Spoon the mixture evenly into the muffin cases. Bake in the oven for 15–20 minutes or until they are light golden brown in colour and an inserted skewer comes out clean. Allow to cool in their tins for 10 minutes and then place on a wire rack to cool completely.

LIQUORICE ICING

100g unsalted butter, at room temperature
400g icing sugar, sifted
40ml star anise milk
½ teaspoon vanilla extract

Place all the ingredients in a large bowl. Using an electric hand-held mixer, mix the ingredients together on a low speed until they are all combined. Then turn up the speed to medium/ high and beat for another 30–45 seconds.

ASSEMBLE

28 whole Liquorice Allsorts, to decorate

Ice each cupcake and decorate with a couple of Liquorice Allsorts on each.

RUM AND RAISIN CUPCAKES

A friend of mine, Ray, really loves rum and raisin ice-cream so he suggested a rum and raisin cupcake. I wasn't sure at first as I am not a huge fan of these flavours, but in fact I was pleasantly surprised. Probably not a cupcake to give to children, this might be nice served after dinner with coffee or even as dessert and could work well alongside mince pies.

Makes 16 regular cupcakes

CUPCAKES

180g raisins (soaked in at least 60ml of dark rum, ideally overnight)
200g unsalted butter, at room temperature
220g soft brown sugar
2 large eggs
1 teaspoon vanilla extract
220g self-raising flour
½ teaspoon salt
90ml milk
40ml dark rum (from soaking the raisins)

Preheat the oven to 180°C/160°C (fan)/gas mark 4. Line two 12-hole muffin tins with 16 muffin cases.

Drain the raisins and reserve the rum (approx. 40ml) in a separate bowl.

Using an electric mixer, cream the butter and sugar in a bowl until light and fluffy. Add the eggs one at a time, beating well after each addition. Add the vanilla extract and beat on a medium speed for about 30 seconds.

Sift in the flour and salt and mix on a low speed until combined and then pour in the milk and reserved rum and mix to combine. If you don't have enough rum from soaking the raisins, top up with extra to make up to 40ml. Add the rum-soaked raisins and fold gently into the batter with a spoon. Divide the mixture evenly between the muffin cases and bake for 18–20 minutes or until golden brown in colour and an inserted skewer comes out clean.

Once the cupcakes have cooled in their tins for about 15 minutes, brush each one with 2 coats of the left-over drained rum from the raisins. Then place on a rack to cool fully.

RUM BUTTERCREAM ICING

130g unsalted butter, at room temperature
4 tablespoons dark rum
400g icing sugar, sifted

Place the butter, rum and half the icing sugar in a bowl. Beat on a low speed until all the ingredients are combined and then add the remaining icing sugar. Beat first on a low speed until thoroughly combined and then finish with a minute of beating on a high speed.

ASSEMBLE

extra raisins, to decorate

Ice each cupcake with some of the icing and decorate with a couple of raisins, either rum-soaked, plain or chocolate-coated.

APPLE CRUMBLE
AND CUSTARD CUPCAKES

It is hard to imagine a more comforting or English dessert for a winter's evening than apple crumble and custard, so a cupcake version was inevitable. After an afternoon decorating the Christmas tree or singing carols, these would be delicious to tuck into.

Makes 21 regular cupcakes

APPLE FILLING

½ tablespoon cornflour
2 teaspoons water
4 medium Granny Smith apples
2 teaspoons ground cinnamon
30g unsalted butter
70g soft brown sugar

To make the apple filling, mix the cornflour and water in a small bowl and set aside.

Peel the apples and dice into roughly 1cm cubes. Put them into a large pan or frying pan. Add the cinnamon, butter and sugar and place over a medium/high heat. Stir the apples regularly and let them simmer for about 3 minutes, until they become slightly translucent.

Pour the cornflour and water mixture into the pan and stir for approximately 30 seconds, then remove the pan from the heat. Set aside to cool.

CUPCAKES

300g unsalted butter, at room temperature
250g soft brown sugar
4 large eggs
320g self-raising flour
2½ teaspoons ground cinnamon
a pinch of salt
70g apple sauce or use extra cooked apple filling
380–420g apple filling

Preheat the oven to 180°C/160°C (fan)/gas mark 4. Line two 12-hole muffin tins with 21 muffin cases.

To make the cupcakes, cream the butter and sugar in a bowl until light and fluffy. Add the eggs one at a time, ensuring each is well combined before adding the next.

Add the flour, cinnamon and salt and mix until just combined. Fold in the apple sauce and cooked apples until everything is well mixed.

Spoon the mixture into the muffin cases and bake in the oven for about 25–30 minutes, or until an inserted skewer comes out clean. Leave in the tins for about 10 minutes, then place on a wire rack to cool completely. Leave the oven on and make the crumble topping while the cakes are cooling.

CRUMBLE TOPPING

100g unsalted butter, chilled
120g soft brown sugar
300g plain flour
2 teaspoons cold water

To make the crumble topping, put the butter, sugar and flour into a bowl. Rub the flour into the mixture with your fingertips until it resembles breadcrumbs. Add the cold water and mix until it is all just combined. Place the mixture in the freezer for 15 minutes.

 Spread the mixture evenly on a baking tray and bake in the oven at the same temperature as the cakes until golden brown – this should take 20–25 minutes.

CUSTARD BUTTERCREAM ICING

170g unsalted butter, at room temperature
50g custard powder
350g icing sugar
4 tablespoons milk

Put all the ingredients into a bowl and beat until combined. The mixture will look like it's slightly split. If it is too sloppy, sift in more icing sugar and beat again.

ASSEMBLE

Ice the cupcakes with the custard buttercream and sprinkle with the crumble topping.

BLUEBERRY CUPCAKES

In the midst of all that chocolate at Christmas, it would be nice to make these richly coloured blueberry cupcakes and pretend for a minute that you are eating something super healthy!

Makes 12 regular cupcakes

BLUEBERRY SYRUP

200g fresh or frozen blueberries
50g golden caster sugar
juice of 1 lemon

Put all the blueberry syrup ingredients into a small pan and bring to the boil on the hob. Turn the heat down and simmer for 1–2 minutes, or until the blueberries are soft. Do not stir too vigorously or the blueberries will break open and lose their shape.

Strain the blueberries over a bowl, then set the blueberries aside (you will be using them in the cupcakes) and return all the liquid to the pan. On a low/medium heat, bring the liquid to a simmer and, stirring regularly, reduce until it is a thick syrup. This will take about 5 minutes. Be careful, as it can burn easily once it starts thickening.

Once the syrup has thickened, pour it into a clean bowl and leave to cool completely before using.

CUPCAKES

170g unsalted butter, at room temperature
210g golden caster sugar
2 large eggs
1 teaspoon vanilla extract
250g self-raising flour
a pinch of salt
whole blueberries, reserved from making the syrup (approx. 140g)

Preheat the oven to 180°C/160°C (fan)/gas mark 4. Line a 12-hole muffin tin with 12 muffin cases.

Using an electric mixer, cream the butter and sugar together in a bowl until light and fluffy. Add the eggs one at a time, beating well after each addition. Add the vanilla with the second egg.

On a low speed, beat in the flour and salt until just combined. Fold in the reserved blueberries with a spatula. Spoon the mixture evenly into the muffin cases, filling them about two-thirds full.

Bake for 15–18 minutes, until golden brown or an inserted skewer comes out clean. Allow to cool in the tin for about 10 minutes, then place on a wire rack to cool completely.

BLUEBERRY ICING

70g unsalted butter, at room temperature
365g icing sugar, sifted
50ml blueberry syrup (see previous page)
20ml milk

Combine all the ingredients in a bowl and beat on a low speed until smooth. Increase to a medium/high speed and beat for a further 30 seconds.

ASSEMBLE

fresh blueberries, to decorate (optional)

Ice the cupcakes with the blueberry icing and either leave undecorated or place a few fresh blueberries on each one.

CINNAMON CUPCAKES

The idea for these cupcakes came from a trip to Arizona in the US in 2013, when I tried some there and wondered why we had never made them at the bakery. The taste and smell of cinnamon reminds many of us of Christmas, and these cupcakes should really please any cinnamon lover.

Makes 15 regular cupcakes

CUPCAKES

220g self-raising flour
2 teaspoons ground cinnamon
a pinch of salt
200g unsalted butter, at room temperature
240g golden caster sugar
2 large eggs
½ teaspoon vanilla extract
160ml sour cream

Preheat the oven to 180°C/160°C (fan)/gas mark 4. Line two 12-hole muffin tins with 15 muffin cases.

Sift the flour, cinnamon and salt together into a bowl and set aside.

Using an electric hand mixer, cream the butter and sugar together for 3–5 minutes, until light and fluffy. Beat in the eggs one at a time, ensuring that each is well combined before adding the next. Add the vanilla extract with the second egg.

Add half the flour mixture and beat on a low speed until combined. Beat half the sour cream into the batter until it is just mixed through. Repeat the steps until all the flour and sour cream have been added.

Spoon the mixture into the muffin cases. Bake for 15–18 minutes, or until an inserted skewer comes out clean. Allow the cupcakes to cool in their tins for about 10 minutes, then place on a wire rack to cool completely.

CINNAMON CREAM CHEESE ICING

100g unsalted butter, at room temperature
450g icing sugar
1½ teaspoons ground cinnamon
220g cream cheese, at room temperature

Put all the ingredients into a large mixing bowl. Mix with an electric hand mixer on a low speed until they are all combined. Turn up the speed to medium/high and continue mixing for about 30 seconds to 1 minute.

Note: Do not overmix the icing, as it will become sloppy and soft. Keep it refrigerated if not using immediately.

CINNAMON SUGAR
(for decoration)

2 tablespoons golden caster sugar
1 tablespoon ground cinnamon

Put the sugar and ground cinnamon into a bowl and stir to combine.

ASSEMBLE

Ice the cupcakes with the cinnamon icing, then sprinkle the cinnamon sugar over each one.

IRISH COFFEE CUPCAKES

Irish coffee is a popular warming cocktail, and this cupcake version would work well either at the end of a pre-Christmas dinner or to take as a contribution to a work party.

Makes 12 regular cupcakes

CUPCAKES

220g plain flour
¼ teaspoon baking powder
½ teaspoon bicarbonate of soda
a pinch of salt
3 tablespoons espresso powder
130g unsalted butter, at room temperature
90g soft light brown sugar
70g golden caster sugar
2 large eggs
1 teaspoon vanilla extract
100ml semi-skimmed milk

Preheat the oven to 180°C/160°C (fan)/gas mark 4. Line a 12-hole muffin tin with 12 muffin cases.

Sift the flour, baking powder, bicarbonate of soda, salt and espresso powder into a bowl and set aside.

Using an electric mixer, cream the butter and sugars together in another bowl until light and fluffy. Add the eggs one at a time, beating well after each addition. Add the vanilla extract with the second egg.

Add half the dry ingredients and beat on a low speed until just combined. Pour in half the milk and beat until just combined. Repeat the previous two steps until all the ingredients have been used.

Divide the batter evenly between the muffin cases, filling them two-thirds full. Bake for 15–18 minutes, until light golden brown or an inserted skewer comes out clean. Allow the cupcakes to cool in their tin for about 10 minutes, then place on a wire rack to cool completely.

BAILEYS COFFEE BUTTERCREAM

75g unsalted butter
375g icing sugar, sifted
½ teaspoon espresso powder
80ml Baileys Irish Coffee Liqueur
  (or whisky)

Put all the ingredients into a bowl. Beat with an electric hand mixer on a low speed until they are all just combined, then increase the speed to medium and beat for a further minute.

ASSEMBLE

Extra espresso powder, to decorate
  (optional)

Ice the cupcakes with the buttercream. Sprinkle with a little espresso powder just before serving.

EGGNOG CUPCAKES

This is a true Christmas cupcake and, unlike some of the others in this chapter, I really can't imagine eating it at any other time. Having said that, the delicious combination of spices and rum in the cupcakes certainly make it a tempting idea for almost any time of year.

Makes 15 regular cupcakes

HOMEMADE EGGNOG

250ml whole milk
½ teaspoon ground nutmeg
a pinch of ground cinnamon
2 whole cloves
a pinch of salt
2 large egg yolks
65g granulated sugar
125ml double cream
25ml dark rum (or to taste)
½ teaspoon vanilla extract

The eggnog needs to be made the day before the cupcakes, or you could use shop-bought eggnog if you are pushed for time. Pour the milk into a small pan and add the spices and salt. Place on the lowest heat possible for 5 minutes, to allow the spices to infuse. Then turn the heat up to medium, bring the milk up to a light simmer, and remove from the heat.

In a bowl, whisk the egg yolks and sugar together until light and fluffy. In a slow and steady stream, pour all the milk on to the egg yolks while whisking. Strain this mixture back into the pan and place over a low/medium heat.

Cook for 3 minutes, stirring constantly, until the mixture is thick – do not allow it to boil. Remove from the heat and leave to cool for at least 30–45 minutes.

Stir in the cream, rum and vanilla, and refrigerate overnight before using. The extra eggnog can be enjoyed while making the cupcakes.

CUPCAKES

220g self-raising flour
1½ teaspoons ground nutmeg
½ teaspoon ground cloves
a pinch of salt
200g unsalted butter, at room temperature
240g golden caster sugar
2 large eggs
1 teaspoon dark rum
160ml eggnog (follow recipe on previous
  page, or buy ready-made in supermarkets
  or online)

Preheat the oven to 180°C/160°C (fan)/gas
mark 4. Line two 12-hole muffin tins with
15 muffin cases.

Sift the flour, nutmeg, cloves and salt into a
bowl and set aside.

Using an electric mixer, cream the butter and
sugar together in another bowl until light and
fluffy. Add the eggs and rum and mix well. Pour
in the dry ingredients and mix until everything
just comes together. Pour in the eggnog and beat
until smooth.

Spoon the batter evenly into the muffin cases
and bake for 18–20 minutes, until a light golden
brown or an inserted skewer comes out clean.
Let the cupcakes cool in their tins for about
10 minutes, then place on a wire rack to cool
completely.

EGGNOG ICING

150g unsalted butter, at room temperature
125ml eggnog (see previous page)
450g icing sugar

To make the icing, combine all the ingredients
in a bowl and beat together until the icing is
smooth and well combined.

ASSEMBLE

extra ground nutmeg, to decorate

Ice the cupcakes with the eggnog icing and
sprinkle a little ground nutmeg over the top
of each one.

S'MORES CUPCAKES

A s'more is an American treat consisting of marshmallow, chocolate and biscuits, sandwiched together and traditionally toasted over a campfire. Both my daughters love them and have eaten them at my father's house in Wales while camping in his garden, so the eldest, Daisy, decided to turn them into a cupcake. This is a nice recipe to make with children on a winter's afternoon before Christmas.

Makes 20 regular cupcakes

CUPCAKES

marshmallow icing (see overleaf)
115g good-quality dark chocolate
  (70% cocoa solids)
85g unsalted butter, at room temperature
175g soft brown sugar
2 large eggs, separated
185g plain flour
¾ teaspoon baking powder
¾ teaspoon bicarbonate of soda
a pinch of salt
250ml semi-skimmed milk, at room
  temperature
1 teaspoon vanilla extract
12 chocolate digestive biscuits, roughly
  chopped, plus extra for sprinkling

Preheat the oven to 180°C/160°C (fan)/gas mark 4. Line two 12-hole muffin tins with 20 muffin cases.

Make the marshmallow icing first (see overleaf) as you will need to use some in the cupcake batter.

For the cupcakes, melt the chocolate (the easiest way is in a microwave – on a medium heat for 1 minute, stir, then microwave again for a further minute – but be very careful not to burn the chocolate!). Leave to cool slightly.

Cream the butter and sugar together, using an electric hand mixer, until pale and smooth. In a separate bowl and with clean beaters, beat the egg yolks for several minutes. Slowly add the egg yolks to the creamed butter and sugar and beat well. Next, add the chocolate and beat well.

Sift together the flour, baking powder, bicarbonate of soda and salt. Combine the milk and vanilla in a jug. Add the flour mixture to the chocolate, butter and sugar, alternating with the milk and vanilla. Beat very well after each addition.

In a clean bowl, whisk the egg whites until soft peaks start to form. Carefully fold the egg whites into the main batter, using a metal spoon. Do not beat or you will take all the air out of the cakes.

Fold the roughly chopped (not too fine) chocolate digestives into the chocolate batter until well combined. Add about one-third of the marshmallow icing to the batter and stir only briefly. The marshmallow icing should not be mixed in thoroughly – streaks of it should still be seen in the cakes. Place the remaining marshmallow icing in the fridge until the cakes are cooked and cooled.

Divide the mixture equally between the prepared cases. You do not need to fill the cases with mixture – about two-thirds full will work best, as the cakes will rise considerably in the oven. The batter will be of a fairly liquid consistency, so take care when spooning it out as it can end up being very messy! You can even use a jug to pour the batter into the cupcake cases if it gets too difficult to spoon.

Place the tins in the oven and bake for 20–25 minutes. Leave the cupcakes in their tins for 10 minutes or so before placing on a wire rack to cool.

MARSHMALLOW ICING

120g granulated sugar
80g golden syrup or light karo syrup
1½ tablespoons water
2 large egg whites
½ teaspoon vanilla extract

Put the sugar, golden syrup and water into a saucepan and cook on a high heat until the mixture reaches soft ball stage – this is when the bubbles in the mixture almost start to stick together and will drop off a spoon in a smooth, slow stream. This could take about up to 6 minutes.

In a clean bowl, whisk the egg whites until soft peaks start to form.

When the mixture reaches soft ball stage, remove from the heat. Using an electric mixer on a low speed, slowly pour the hot sugar mixture in a slow, steady stream into the egg whites. Continue to beat on a low speed until all the hot sugar is in the mixing bowl.

Turn the mixer up to medium/high speed and continue whipping the mixture until it becomes thick, glossy and cool. Add the vanilla towards the end of the mixing process.

Please note that this buttercream is easiest to work with while it is still a bit warm, so try to use it right away. If you do have some left over, you can store it in the fridge overnight, but we would not recommend keeping the unused icing for long.

ASSEMBLE

To assemble the cupcakes, ice them with the marshmallow icing.

If you have a cook's blowtorch (which is actually quite a handy and fun kitchen gadget to have on the odd occasion), flame the icing quickly to give it some colour (almost as if it has been scorched by the campfire). Be careful not to burn the icing.

Sprinkle each cupcake with chopped chocolate digestives and serve immediately.

MARASCHINO CHERRY CUPCAKES ✳

Maraschino cherries are more commonly used in cocktails or as a garnish on desserts and cakes, but their bright red colour and sweet taste make for some fun Christmas cupcakes that will brighten up any table.

Makes 12 regular cupcakes

CUPCAKES

150g unsalted butter, at room temperature
150g granulated sugar
4 large eggs
1 ½ teaspoons vanilla extract
¾ teaspoon almond extract
225g self-raising flour
a pinch of salt
3 tablespoons maraschino cherry syrup
  (from the jar of cherries – see below)
24 maraschino cherries, from a jar
red food colouring

Preheat the oven to 180°C/160°C (fan)/gas mark 4. Line a 12-hole muffin tin with 12 muffin cases.

Cream the butter and sugar with an electric hand mixer until it is pale and light and fluffy. Add the eggs one at a time, ensuring each is combined before adding the next. Add the vanilla and almond extracts with the last egg.

Sift in the flour and salt and mix on a low speed until just combined. Pour in the cherry syrup and a few drops of red food colouring and mix until the batter is smooth and pale pink in colour.

Fill each muffin case about two-thirds full and place a cherry in each one. Bake for 15–18 minutes, until golden brown or an inserted skewer comes out clean. Leave to cool in their tin for about 10 minutes, then place on a wire rack to cool completely.

ASSEMBLE

1 x batch of marshmallow icing (see page 64)

Ice the cupcakes with the marshmallow icing and top with the remaining maraschino cherries. Serve immediately.

RED BEAN CUPCAKES

Red, or azuki, beans are grown widely across East Asia, where they are commonly used in desserts and cakes once they have been sweetened and turned into a paste. We decided to try a cupcake version – we have both a Japanese and a Thai chef and we wanted to make something that would remind them of home, especially when they are unable to get back there for Christmas. You should be able to find both azuki beans and red bean paste either online or in more specialist Japanese and Chinese food stores.

Makes 12 regular cupcakes

COOKED RED BEANS
(makes approx. 120g)

50g red (azuki) beans
900ml water
25g golden caster sugar

Wash the beans and drain in a colander. Place the beans in a bowl, cover with cold water and leave to soak for 6–8 hours, preferably overnight. Drain the beans, then put them in a pan with 250ml of the water and bring to the boil over a high heat. Once boiling, add another 100ml of water and keep boiling for a further 5 minutes.

Drain the beans, then put them back into the pan. Pour the remaining water into the pan and bring to the boil again over a high heat. Once the water starts boiling, reduce the heat and simmer until the beans are soft, topping up the water if necessary. This will take approximately 50–60 minutes.

Drain the beans, return to the pan and mix with the sugar over a low heat. Set aside to cool.

CUPCAKES

150g unsalted butter, at room temperature
150g golden caster sugar
3 large eggs
150g self-raising flour
a pinch of salt
225g red bean paste
110g cooked red beans (see opposite)

Preheat the oven to 180°C/160°C (fan)/gas mark 4. Line a 12-hole muffin tin with 12 muffin cases.

Using an electric hand mixer, cream the butter and sugar together until light and fluffy. Add the eggs to the bowl one at a time, ensuring each one is well mixed in before adding the next. Add the flour and salt and mix on a low speed until everything is just combined.

Gently fold the red bean paste and the cooked red beans into the batter, using a spoon or spatula.

Divide the mixture evenly between the cases, filling each one about two-thirds full. Bake in the oven for about 20–25 minutes, or until light golden brown and an inserted skewer comes out clean. Let the cupcakes cool in their tin for about 10 minutes, then place on a wire rack to cool completely.

RED BEAN AND CREAM CHEESE ICING

70g red bean paste
50g cream cheese, softened or at room temperature
35g unsalted butter, at room temperature
210g icing sugar

Put all the ingredients into a bowl and mix on a low speed until everything comes together. Then beat for a further 30–60 seconds on a medium/high speed until very smooth and creamy.

ASSEMBLE

Ice the cupcakes with the red bean and cream cheese icing. Store any unused icing in the fridge.

BREAD AND BUTTER PUDDING CUPCAKES

This is one of our newest cupcakes and I think you will like it even if you do not love bread and butter pudding, especially with this caramelised creamy butter icing.

Makes 20 regular cupcakes

CUPCAKES

225ml semi-skimmed milk
225ml double cream
300g white sliced bread, with crusts removed,
  cut into small cubes
4 eggs, lightly beaten
100g golden caster sugar
100g unsalted butter, melted
2 teaspoons vanilla extract
40g plain flour
1½ teaspoons baking powder
½ teaspoon ground cinnamon
100g raisins
1 apple, peeled, cored and diced into
  1cm cubes
zest of 1 lemon

Preheat the oven to 180°C/160°C (fan)/gas mark 4. Line two 12-hole muffin tins with 20 muffin cases.

Pour the milk and cream into a bowl and add the bread cubes. Stir together until all the bread is coated and leave for about 10 minutes to soak.

Mix the eggs, sugar, butter and vanilla into the bread mixture. Add the flour, baking powder and cinnamon and fold until combined. Fold in the raisins, apple and lemon zest.

Scoop the mixture evenly into the muffin cases and bake for 25–30 minutes until they are a light golden brown. Allow to cool for 15 minutes, then remove from their tins and leave to cool completely on a wire rack.

BEURRE NOISETTE ICING

For the beurre noisette (brown butter/hazelnut butter)
270g unsalted butter, cut into small cubes

To make the beurre noisette, put 120g of the butter into a heavy-based pan over a medium heat. Melt the butter and stir with a whisk. The butter will start to foam, but it will subside during cooking. Do not leave the pan unattended, as the butter burns very easily and quickly. Heat until it starts to turn golden brown (beurre noisette stage), then remove from the heat and place the base of the pan in a bowl of cold water for about 20 seconds, stirring. Gradually add the rest of the butter a third at a time, making sure the butter has melted before you add any more. Once made, put the beurre noisette into a container and into the fridge.

For the icing
3 egg whites
¼ teaspoon cream of tartar
24g granulated sugar
95g demerara sugar
24ml water
beurre noisette (see above), at room temperature
1 teaspoon vanilla extract

To make the icing, take the beurre noisette out of the fridge and allow it to come to room temperature.

Using an electric mixer, whisk the egg whites and cream of tartar on a medium/high speed until they form soft peaks. Gradually pour in the granulated sugar while continuing to whisk on a medium speed. Keep whisking until stiff peaks are formed.

Combine the demerara sugar and water in a pan and bring to the boil. Boil for about 4 minutes (or using a candy thermometer, bring it to 118°C). Once the sugar syrup is ready, start the mixer on a low/medium speed and pour the syrup into the egg whites in a slow and steady stream. Once it has all been added, whisk on a high speed until the mixture has cooled.

With the mixer on a medium speed, add small amounts of the beurre noisette to the egg whites, allowing each addition to be fully incorporated before adding the next. Finally add the vanilla and beat together to get a creamy icing.

ASSEMBLE

Ice the cooled cupcakes with the beurre noisette icing and serve.

LARGE CAKES

Christmas is definitely a time to make and eat any one of the cakes in this chapter. There would be nothing nicer than a cosy tea with a table piled high with sandwiches, crumpets, biscuits and one of these cakes as the centrepiece.

We have used flavours that remind us of Christmas and are sometimes more easily available then, and that are perhaps a little richer and more indulgent than you might enjoy at other times of the year. We have also included recipes that are particularly popular at Christmas in different parts of the world – although Primrose Bakery is quintessentially British, our origins and inspiration are much more international, and one of the nicest things about the bakery is the huge variety of nationalities we have employed in the last ten years and what we have learnt from them.

These cakes might on the whole be a little more time-consuming than many of our other cakes. Please don't be put off, as they will all be more than worth trying out, and we feel that at Christmas there is usually a little more time to spend baking and preparing something spectacular.

RAINBOW CAKE

This is one of our favourite new cakes, with its rainbow of sponge colours. It would make a fantastic birthday cake, especially for a Christmas birthday, where its colours will really make it stand out on the table. Be patient when making it, as it is more time-consuming and fiddly than a simple two-layer cake but well worth the effort.

Makes one 20cm cake with 5 layers, serving 12–15

SPONGE

420g self-raising flour
450g golden caster sugar
50g cornflour
2 teaspoons baking powder
450g unsalted butter, at room temperature
8 large eggs
6 tablespoons semi-skimmed milk
2 teaspoons good-quality vanilla extract
½ teaspoon each pink, lilac, blue, green and yellow food colouring

Preheat the oven to 180°C/160°C (fan)/gas mark 4. Grease five 20cm sandwich cake tins and line the base of each tin with some baking or parchment paper.

To make the sponge, sift the flour, sugar, cornflour and baking powder into a food processor and process for about 20 seconds. Add the remaining ingredients, apart from the food colouring, and process briefly. Don't be tempted to leave the processor on and walk away, as the batter will quickly overmix, resulting in a heavier-textured cake.

Divide the batter evenly between 5 bowls and add a colour to each one. Stir the food colouring in gently until it is all mixed through, but do not overwork the batter. Pour the batter into the lined tins and smooth the tops with a spatula.

Bake in the oven for about 15–20 minutes, until the cakes have risen and an inserted skewer comes out clean. Leave the cakes to cool slightly in their tins for about 10 minutes, then turn out on to wire racks and leave to cool completely.

Once the cakes are cool, remove the baking paper circles and lay one cake on a plate or cake board. If any of the cakes are domed, trim the top to ensure they are all as flat as possible before stacking.

VANILLA BUTTERCREAM

460g unsalted butter, at room temperature
240ml semi-skimmed milk
4 teaspoons good-quality vanilla extract
2kg icing sugar, sifted

Using an electric hand mixer, beat the butter, milk, vanilla extract and half the icing sugar in a bowl until smooth. This will usually take a few minutes. Gradually add the remainder of the icing sugar to produce a buttercream with a creamy smooth consistency. The buttercream can be stored in an airtight container for up to 3 days at room temperature. Beat well again before re-using.

ASSEMBLE

To assemble the cake, spread a thin layer of vanilla buttercream on the top of the first cake (you can decide which order you want the colours to go) and place the second cake carefully on top. Continue until all five cakes are stacked on top of each other. Place the whole cake in the fridge for about 15–20 minutes to allow the buttercream to set. Remove from the fridge and crumb coat the cake by spreading a thin layer of buttercream down the sides and over the top of the cake. This will ensure no crumbs will fall away from the cake when the final layer of buttercream is spread on top later. Place the cake in the fridge for about 30 minutes, or until the buttercream is chilled and set when touched. Once set, use the remaining butter-cream to spread around the sides and top of the cake to hide the colours of the cake layers. Finish by decorating in whatever way you would like – coloured sprinkles look nice.

SALTED CARAMEL CHEESECAKE

Salted caramel is one of the most popular flavours at the bakery, and we think you can never have too much of it. Here it is used to make a cheesecake, which could be served as a delicious pre-Christmas dessert.

Makes one 25cm cake, serving up to 20

CARAMELISED PECANS

20 pecan nut halves
100g white granulated sugar

First make the caramelised pecans. Place the pecans close together on a lined baking tray and set aside. Gently heat the sugar in a heavy-based pan on the hob until the sugar has melted and is a pale golden colour. Pour the melted sugar over the pecans, covering them completely. Leave to cool.

Now make the caramel sauce.

SALTED CARAMEL SAUCE

110g granulated sugar
3 tablespoons water
125ml double cream
1 teaspoon fleur de sel

Note: This is a very hot liquid, so please be careful when making it.

Put the sugar and water in a clean medium pan. Place it over a medium heat on the hob. Do not stir as this will cause the sugar syrup to crystallise. Swirl the pan occasionally and gently until all the sugar has dissolved. Then turn the heat up to high and let the syrup boil until it becomes a lovely caramel colour.

While the sugar syrup is boiling, pour the cream into a separate pan and add the fleur de sel. Heat gently for about a minute, to take the chill off it, and then remove from the heat. Do not allow it to boil.

Once the sugar syrup is off the heat, immediately add a small portion of the warmed cream. Stir quickly with a wooden spoon to prevent it from sticking to the bottom of the pan. Be careful when adding the cream, as it will bubble up and rise very quickly and let off a lot of hot steam and may splutter. Add the remainder of the cream in small amounts. Keep stirring while the cream is being added.

Pour the sauce into a bowl and set it aside to cool.

CHEESECAKE BASE

300g Rich Tea biscuits
150g unsalted butter, melted
10 caramelised pecans

To make the base, grease a 25cm, ideally springform, cake tin and line with parchment paper. Place the biscuits and caramelised pecans into a food processor and pulse until they resemble breadcrumbs. Place in a large bowl, then pour in the melted butter and mix until it is thoroughly combined. Press this mixture evenly into the base of the tin. Put it into the fridge to set while you prepare the filling.

CHEESECAKE FILLING

600ml boiling water
550g cream cheese, softened
200g golden caster sugar
2 eggs
1 teaspoon vanilla extract
80g butter, melted
150ml sour cream

Preheat the oven to 160°C/140°C (fan)/gas mark 3. Pour 600ml of boiling water into a roasting tin and place it on the bottom rack of the oven.

Put the cream cheese and sugar into a bowl and, using an electric mixer, beat until smooth and well combined. Add the eggs, vanilla, melted butter and sour cream and mix until all the ingredients are combined.

ASSEMBLE

To assemble the cheesecake, pour the filling on top of the chilled base in the cake tin and spread it out evenly with a spatula. Drizzle

3 tablespoons of salted caramel sauce on top of the filling. Using a skewer, gently swirl the sauce into the filling to create a marbled effect.

Place the tin on the middle rack of the oven, above the pan of hot water. Bake in the oven for 30 minutes, then remove the pan of hot water from the oven.

Turn the heat down to 150°C/130°C (fan)/gas mark 2 and bake for a further 30–40 minutes, or until the top is set, light golden brown in colour and an inserted skewer comes out clean. If the cheesecake starts to brown before it has set, cover it with foil to prevent further browning.

Once you have removed the cheesecake from the oven, let it cool in the tin. Then put it into the fridge to chill, preferably overnight.

FINISH AND SERVE

To serve, drizzle some more of the salted caramel sauce on top. Roughly chop the rest of the caramelised pecans and sprinkle them all over the cheesecake.

APPLE AND BUTTERSCOTCH YULE LOG

Apple and butterscotch are such great flavours when combined, especially in this Yule log, which you could decorate with some real holly or plastic or sugar Christmas cake decorations

Makes one log, serving 6–8 people

SPONGE

85g self-raising flour
4 large eggs, separated
75g golden caster sugar

Preheat the oven to 180°C/160°C (fan)/gas mark 4.

Lightly grease a Swiss roll tin (25 x 38cm) and line with parchment paper.

Sift the flour into a bowl and set aside.

Using an electric hand mixer, beat the egg yolks and sugar together in another bowl until pale and thick and resembling ribbons when you lift the mixers out. Sift the flour again on to the top of the egg yolk mixture. Fold in gently with a spatula.

In a clean bowl, beat the egg whites until they just reach stiff peaks. Add a third of the egg whites to the egg yolk mixture and fold in gently. Add the remaining egg whites and fold in until they are all incorporated.

Pour the mixture straight into the prepared tin and spread it out evenly. Bake for 6–8 minutes, until light golden brown and firm to touch. Do not overcook, as it will crack when rolling. Let it cool in the tin for 2 minutes, then remove and place on a wire rack to cool completely. Cover with a tea towel while cooling.

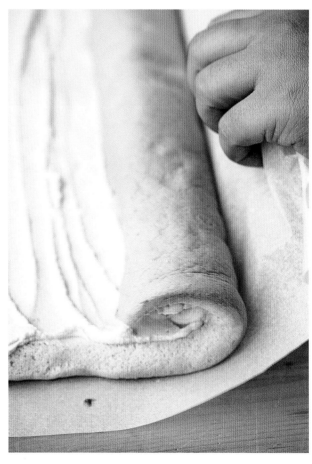

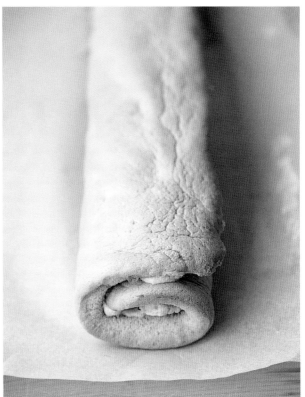

CARAMEL APPLES

**2 Granny Smith apples, peeled and
cut into 1cm cubes**
50g soft light brown sugar
½ tablespoon unsalted butter

For the caramel apples, place the butter, sugar
and cubes of apple in a pan and cook on a high
heat until transparent and slightly soft. This will
probably take around 10–15 minutes. Remove
from the heat and set aside to cool completely.

BUTTERSCOTCH CREAM

200g soft light brown sugar
100g unsalted butter
450ml double cream
50g icing sugar, sifted

For the butterscotch cream, place the sugar,
butter and 150ml of double cream in a pan and
bring to the boil. Reduce the heat and let the
mixture simmer for 5–8 minutes until it is thick.
Remove from the heat, pour it into a large bowl
and let it cool completely. Put the remaining
300ml of double cream and the icing sugar into a
clean bowl and beat until it forms medium peaks.
Fold this cream gently into the cooled sauce until
well incorporated.

ASSEMBLE

To assemble the Yule log, cut a piece of parchment paper the length of the cake. Flip the cake
out on to the paper, then carefully remove the
baked piece of parchment paper.

Spread a thin layer of butterscotch cream over
the cake, all the way to the edges. Spoon the
cooled apples in a mound lengthways along one
side of the cake, about 2cm from the edge. The
apples should be along the edge closest to you.

Lift the cake and start wrapping it around the
apples. Keep rolling the cake until the other end
is reached. Try to get a tight roll in the beginning
so that the apples will stay intact.

Using a serrated knife, cut off either one or
both ends of the cake at an angle, about 5–6cm
in length. These will make the branches of the log.

Move the large log on to a cake board or plate,
securing it with a little cream on the underside.
Place the cut-off pieces on the main log at an
angle, to look as though the branches are coming
off the log. To secure, place some cream on
the ends touching the main log and push them
in lightly.

Cover the whole log with the remaining cream
and use a palette knife or skewer to create the
wood/bark texture.

CHOCOLATE AND COCONUT LAYER CAKE ✳

Chocolate and coconut are a good flavour combination, and this would make a good alternative to a traditional chocolate cake. The black and white stripy layers look pretty and elegant on any tea table.

Makes one rectangular 4-layer cake, serving 8–10

SPONGE

40g self-raising flour
50g cornflour
6 large eggs, separated
200g golden caster sugar
220g dark chocolate (70% cocoa solids), melted

Preheat the oven to 180°C/160°C (fan)/gas mark 4.

Lightly grease a Swiss roll tin (25 x 38cm) and line with parchment paper.

Sift the flours into a bowl and set aside.

In another bowl, beat the egg yolks and half the sugar together until the mixture is pale and has a ribbon-like texture. Pour in the melted chocolate and gently fold it in with a spatula.

In a clean bowl beat the egg whites and remaining sugar together until the mixture is shiny and reaches medium peaks. Fold a third of the mixture into the chocolate and egg yolk mixture.

Add the flours and gently fold in with a spatula. Add the remaining egg white mixture and fold gently again. Be careful not to knock out too much of the air from the egg whites.

Pour this mixture into the tin and spread out evenly.

Bake on the middle rack of the oven for 10–12 minutes, until an inserted skewer comes out clean. Leave in its tin for about 5 minutes, then remove and transfer the cake (including the paper) on to a wire rack to cool completely.

COCONUT AND WHITE CHOCOLATE ICING

90g unsalted butter, at room temperature
200g icing sugar, sifted
80g desiccated coconut
50ml coconut milk
100g white chocolate, melted and cooled

Place the butter, icing sugar, desiccated coconut and coconut milk in a bowl. With an electric mixer, beat on a low/medium speed until the mixture is smooth. Add the white chocolate and beat for a further 30 seconds.

ASSEMBLE

To assemble, slice the sponge into 4 equal rectangles. Placing a layer of coconut icing between each slice of cake, stack to make a rectangular layer cake.

✳ CHRISTMAS PAVLOVA WREATH

A pavlova is one of the best-loved and most widely eaten desserts in Australia and New Zealand, especially at Christmas time, which falls in their summer months, although there is some debate over which of them was the first to produce it. Given the bakery's links to Australia and New Zealand it seemed natural to include it here, and the combination of meringue, cream and fruit really makes for an amazing Christmas dessert.

Makes one circular pavlova, serving 15–20

PAVLOVA

300g caster sugar
5 egg whites
600ml double or whipping cream
2 heaped tablespoons icing sugar
seasonal fruit to decorate, such as cranberries, redcurrants, clementines (peeled and broken into segments) and cherries (stoned and halved)
a little icing sugar, to dust (optional)

Preheat the oven to 180°C/160°C (fan)/gas mark 4.

Tip the sugar on to a lined baking tray and place in the oven.

While the sugar is heating, start to whisk the egg whites using a stand or hand mixer on a low speed. Once the egg whites start to go foamy/frothy, increase the speed and whisk until firm peaks start to form (this should take about 5 minutes).

Remove the sugar from the oven – it should have just started to melt at the edges.

Turn the oven down to 100°C/80°C (fan)/gas mark ¼.

Add the sugar to the egg whites, a tablespoon at a time, while continuing to whisk. Continue whisking for another 5 minutes, until the meringue mixture is thick and glossy.

Line a square baking tray with parchment paper and place a clean empty jam jar (without its lid) in the centre. Spoon the meringue around the jar, then smooth with a palette knife to create a wreath shape.

Bake in the oven for 2 hours, until the meringue is dry and can easily be removed without breaking.

Leave to cool in the oven with the door ajar for an hour before removing the jam jar from the centre. Once you have removed the jar, transfer the pavlova to a serving dish and leave to cool in the oven overnight.

Whisk the double cream with the icing sugar until it has a a medium to stiff consistency. A tablespoon of brandy could also be added for a variation.

ASSEMBLE

Spread the cream all over the top of the wreath, then decorate with the fruits and dust with icing sugar to finish, if you wish.

PINEAPPLE AND COCONUT CAKE

This is Primrose Bakery's version of a hummingbird cake – these tropical flavours will brighten up a cold Christmas period and bring some much-needed variation to the traditional Christmas foods.

Makes one 25cm cake, serving 15–20

SPONGE

260g plain flour
1½ teaspoons bicarbonate of soda
¼ teaspoon salt
1 teaspoon ground cinnamon
1 teaspoon ground nutmeg
½ teaspoon ground allspice
4 large eggs
200g golden caster sugar
1 teaspoon vanilla extract
200ml vegetable oil
1 ripe banana, mashed
1 tin of pineapple chunks, drained (about 300g)
60g walnut halves, roughly chopped
60g pecan halves, roughly chopped

Preheat the oven to 180°C/160°C (fan)/gas mark 4. Grease and line a deep 25cm cake tin. Sift the flour, bicarbonate of soda, salt and spices into a bowl and set aside.

Put the eggs, sugar and vanilla in a separate bowl and beat with an electric mixer until the mixture is pale and fluffy. While beating, pour the vegetable oil slowly into the mixture in a thin stream.

Add all the sifted dry ingredients and beat on a low speed until the batter is just combined. Fold in the remaining ingredients by hand, using a rubber spatula.

Pour the batter into the prepared tin and bake for 40–50 minutes on the middle shelf of the oven. When cooked, an inserted skewer should come out clean and the cake should be golden brown in colour. Allow to cool in the tin, then turn out carefully on to a wire rack to cool completely. Remove the paper from the base of the cake.

COCONUT ICING

65g unsalted butter
120g cream cheese
600g icing sugar, sifted
80ml coconut milk
30g fine desiccated coconut, plus extra for sprinkling on top

Put all the icing ingredients in a bowl and beat on a low speed until combined. Increase to a medium/high speed and beat for a further 30 seconds.

ASSEMBLE

Ice the top and sides of the cake with the coconut icing. To finish, sprinkle the top with desiccated coconut.

PAIN D'EPICES BUNDT CAKE

Our former chef, Lisa Chan, was keen to make this cake. She had eaten it in France, from where it originates, and she felt the ingredients and taste were very Christmas-like. Normally made as a loaf, this 'spice bread', as it translates, works equally well here as a bundt cake and looks even more festive.

Makes one 20cm bundt cake, serving 10–12

120g unsalted butter
110ml honey
1 teaspoon vanilla extract
zest of 1 orange
80ml semi-skimmed milk
3 large eggs
3 pieces of stem ginger, roughly chopped
140g dark brown sugar
100g plain flour
85g wholemeal flour
1 teaspoon bicarbonate of soda
½ teaspoon baking powder
¼ teaspoon salt
2 teaspoons ground cinnamon
1½ teaspoons ground ginger
½ teaspoon ground nutmeg
½ teaspoon ground cloves
¼ teaspoon ground allspice
stem ginger syrup, to glaze

Preheat the oven to 160°C/140°F/gas mark 3. Lightly grease and flour a 20cm bundt cake tin and set aside.

Place the butter, honey, vanilla and orange zest in a microwaveable bowl or in a small pan and heat on low until the butter has melted. Remove from the heat and set aside to cool slightly.

Add the milk, eggs and chopped stem ginger and mix with a wooden spoon or electric mixer until well combined. Stir in the brown sugar.

Sift all the remaining dry ingredients into a large bowl and make a well in the centre. Pour the liquid mixture into the dry ingredients and combine gently using the low speed of a mixer until you have a smooth batter.

Pour the batter into the cake tin and bake on the middle shelf of the oven for 35–45 minutes, until the cake is a golden brown colour and an inserted skewer comes out clean.

Once you have removed the cake from the oven, leave it in the tin for 15 minutes, then gently turn it out on to a wire rack to cool. Brush with some stem ginger syrup immediately after turning out on to the rack, as it will soak into the sponge more while it is still a little warm. This cake would actually be nice served slightly warm.

CHRISTMAS PUDDING CAKE WITH MULLED WINE ICING

Christmas isn't Christmas without a Christmas pudding, so we couldn't really do a Christmas book and leave all mention of it out. Our head chef, Daniel, has made his variation of it, as a cake with a mulled wine buttercream icing – delicious!

Makes one 25cm cake, serving 15–20

HOMEMADE MULLED WINE

250ml red wine
2 cinnamon sticks
6 cloves
zest of 1 orange

If you are making your own mulled wine, heat the wine in a pan with all the spices, until it just comes to the boil. Remove from the heat, cover and leave to infuse for at least 30 minutes. Strain before using.

CAKE

450g dried fruit (we recommend 200g raisins, 100g cranberries, 100g cherries and 50g mixed peel)
150ml mulled wine (see above, or buy it ready-made)
25ml brandy
25ml rum
300g unsalted butter, at room temperature
300g dark brown sugar
6 large eggs
240g plain flour
1 teaspoon baking powder
1 teaspoon mixed spice
100g ground almonds

Preheat the oven to 180°C/160°C (fan)/gas mark 4. Grease and line a deep 25cm baking tin. Place the dried fruit and alcohol in a pan and

heat them until all the liquid has been absorbed into the fruit. Leave to cool completely.

Cream together the butter and sugar until light and fluffy. Add the eggs one at a time, ensuring that each one is thoroughly mixed in before adding the next.

Combine all the remaining dry ingredients in a separate bowl, then add to the egg and sugar mix, a third at a time, making sure all the flour is mixed in, with no lumps. Fold in the cooled fruit, using a spatula.

Spoon the mixture into the prepared tin and bake in the centre of the oven for about 45–60 minutes, until an inserted skewer comes out clean. Allow to cool in the tin for about 15 minutes, then turn out on to a wire rack to cool completely. Remove the paper from the base of the cake.

MULLED WINE ICING

160g unsalted butter, at room temperature
500g icing sugar, sifted
zest of 1 orange
4 tablespoons mulled wine

Mix the butter, icing sugar, orange zest and half the mulled wine until it all starts to come together. Add the rest of the mulled wine and beat until smooth and fluffy.

ASSEMBLE

Ice the top of the cake with the mulled wine icing and add some berries or other choice of decoration.

‘JAFFA CAKE’ CAKE

It's one of the most loved of biscuits, and we wanted to create a cake version. So Daniel worked on developing one and this was the result. It really does taste like a Jaffa cake!

Makes one 20cm single layer cake, serving 10–12

You will need two 20cm cake tins, one of them fairly deep.

This cake is best prepared a day in advance. That way the jelly has enough time to set, the sponge will be cool and easier to cut, and the ganache will be at the right temperature so that on the day of serving all you have to do is assemble and ice the cake.

ORANGE JELLY

juice of 5 oranges
juice of 1 lime
100g golden caster sugar
7 leaves of gelatine, soaked in cold water

Prepare the jelly in advance to make sure it is properly set. To do this, put all the juice and the sugar into a pan and heat until barely simmering – do not boil! It only needs to be warm enough to dissolve the gelatine. Add the gelatine and stir until no lumps remain. Pour into a 20cm tin lined with cling film and leave in the fridge to set, preferably overnight.

ORANGE SPONGE

250g unsalted butter, at room temperature
300g golden caster sugar
4 large eggs
300g plain flour
2 teaspoons baking powder
zest of 5 oranges
zest of 1 lime
100g natural yoghurt

To make the sponge, preheat the oven to 180°C/160°C (fan)/gas mark 4 and grease and line a deep 20cm cake tin with parchment paper. In a bowl, cream together the butter and sugar until light and fluffy. Add the eggs one at a time, making sure that each one is thoroughly mixed in before adding the next one.

In a separate bowl, mix the flour, baking powder and zests. Add this to the egg and sugar mix a third at a time, making sure it is thoroughly mixed after each addition. Finally add the yoghurt and beat well until it all comes together.

Pour into the prepared tin and bake for 45–60 minutes, until the cake is golden in colour and an inserted skewer comes out clean. Allow to cool in the tin for about 15 minutes, then turn out on to a wire rack to cool completely. Remember to remove the paper from the base.

DARK CHOCOLATE GANACHE

600ml double cream
400g dark chocolate
200g milk chocolate

Pour the cream into a pan and heat until just simmering, but do not allow to boil. Break up the chocolates in a bowl and pour the heated cream over the top. Mix with a spatula until combined and melted. Leave to cool at room temperature until it becomes a good consistency for covering the cake. It should look rich and glossy.

ASSEMBLE

apricot jam
orange zest, to decorate (optional)

To assemble the cake, place your sponge on a cake board or plate. Trim the top so that it is level, then brush with a little apricot jam. This will help the jelly to stick. Carefully remove the jelly from the tin, still in the cling film, and place directly on top of the sponge so that it all lines up, before peeling off the film. Ice the sides of the cake first with some of the ganache, then the top, making sure no sponge or jelly can be seen.

If you want to decorate the cake, scatter some fresh orange zest over the top.

CLEMENTINE CAKE WITH GREEK YOGHURT ICING

From the clementines that were always found in the toe of my Christmas stocking to eating them non-stop through the winter months, this fruit also gives a cake a lovely fresh citrus taste.

Makes one 20cm cake, serving 10–12

SPONGE

3–4 clementines, thinly sliced (peel on), ends removed and retained for the glaze
230g unsalted butter, at room temperature
115g golden caster sugar
115g light brown sugar
3 large eggs
zest of 3 clementines (the juice and flesh will be used to make the glaze)
350g self-raising flour
a pinch of ground cloves
115g Greek yoghurt

Preheat the oven to 180°C/160° (fan)/gas mark 4. Grease a deep 20cm baking tin and line with parchment paper. Line the sides of the tin with the thinly sliced clementines.

Cream the butter and sugars together in a bowl until light and fluffy. Add the eggs, ensuring each one is thoroughly mixed in before adding the next. Add the zest of the clementines, the flour and ground cloves and and beat until combined.

Pour in the yoghurt and mix until smooth.

Pour the batter into the tin and push it out to the edges to ensure the clementines stay upright. Place in the oven and bake for 45 minutes, or until an inserted skewer comes out clean.

Once cooked, remove the cake from the tin, pierce several times with a skewer and set aside.

GLAZE

**juice and flesh of the zested clementines
(see opposite)**
ends of sliced clementines (see opposite)
200g granulated sugar
100ml water

To make the glaze, juice the 3 clementines and
roughly chop them. Place in a pan along with
the ends of the sliced clementines. Mash with a
wooden spoon to get all the juice out of them,
then add the sugar and water. Heat until boiling
and the liquid has reduced to a thick syrup
consistency.

  Remove from the heat and strain the syrup into
a bowl, using a sieve to catch the pulp. Leave
to cool. Once the syrup and cake are cool, use
a pastry brush to cover the cake, including
the sides, with the glaze until it has all been
absorbed by the sponge, keeping some back
for decorating.

GREEK YOGHURT ICING

100g unsalted butter, at room temperature
400g icing sugar, sifted
80g Greek yoghurt

Beat the butter in a bowl until light and fluffy.
Add the icing sugar and yoghurt and beat until
smooth.

ASSEMBLE

reserved glaze

Place the cake on a plate or cake board and
spread the icing all over the top. Finish with
the rest of the glaze, drizzled all over.

CHOCOLATE AND
WHITE CHOCOLATE ROULADE

A classic Christmas dessert, especially for those people who are not so keen on Christmas pudding and would much rather have something involving chocolate (I am one of them).

Makes one roulade, serving 8–10

SPONGE

60g dark chocolate (70% cocoa solids at least)
6 large eggs, separated
100g granulated sugar
40g cocoa powder, plus extra for dusting
25g cornflour

Preheat the oven to 180°C/160°C (fan)/ gas mark 4. Lightly grease a Swiss roll tin (25 x 38cm) and line it with parchment paper.

In a heatproof bowl, melt the chocolate over a pan of simmering water on the hob or in a suitable bowl in the microwave until it is smooth and lump-free. Set aside to cool slightly.

Put the egg yolks and sugar into a bowl and beat until they reach a ribbon-like texture. Pour in the cooled, melted chocolate and fold it in gently with a rubber spatula.

Sift the cocoa powder and cornflour directly on top of the chocolate mixture and fold in gently.

In a separate clean bowl, whisk the egg whites until stiff but not dry. Spoon one-third of the egg whites into the chocolate mixture and, using a metal spoon or a rubber spatula, fold it in gently, to lighten the mix. Fold in the remaining egg whites. This step must be done gently, as you do not want to knock out the air incorporated into the egg whites.

Pour this mixture into the prepared tin and spread it out gently, making sure it is level. Bake in the oven for 12–15 minutes, until the cake is firm to touch and an inserted skewer comes out clean. Be careful not to overcook.

Once removed from the oven, dust the top of

the chocolate cake with some cocoa powder and allow it to cool completely.

WHITE CHOCOLATE CREAM

80g white chocolate
300ml double or whipping cream
½ teaspoon vanilla extract

Place the white chocolate in a heatproof bowl and melt over a pan of simmering water on the hob or melt in a suitable bowl in the microwave until it is smooth. Set aside to cool.

In a clean bowl whip the cream and vanilla together until medium peaks form. Place a couple of spoonfuls of this into the cooled white chocolate and fold in, to lighten the chocolate.

Add the remaining cream and fold in until well combined. The cream should hold its shape – if it doesn't, continue whisking until it has the correct consistency. Be careful not to overwhisk.

Cover the bowl with cling film and place in the fridge while waiting for the cake to cool.

ASSEMBLE

icing sugar, chocolate shavings or fresh berries, to decorate

To assemble, place a clean piece of parchment paper on top of the cooled cake and flip it out on to a large clean surface.

Carefully peel off the paper from the bottom of the cake. Spread the white chocolate cream generously on to the surface and all the way out to the edges of the cake.

With the shortest edge facing you, roll the cake away from you, using the clean parchment paper as a rolling aid. Don't worry if it cracks slightly. Lift carefully on to a serving plate.

Decorate with a dusting of icing sugar, chocolate shavings or fresh berries, as you wish.

You can keep any uneaten roulade in the fridge for a couple of days.

MARJOLAINE CAKE

This cake originates from France and basically involves layers of meringue, chocolate, hazelnuts and cream. It is quite a different style of cake from those we normally make at Primrose Bakery, but our lovely chef Mary wanted to try out a variation and we felt the flavours were very appropriate for Christmas and it would be quite nice to have something a little bit different from normal.

Makes one triple-layer 20cm cake, serving 12–15

HAZELNUT SPONGE

3 egg whites
150g icing sugar
3 large eggs
150g ground hazelnuts
50g plain flour
25g unsalted butter, melted

Preheat the oven to 180°C/160°C (fan)/gas mark 4. Lightly grease and line the base of three 20cm cake tins.

In a clean bowl, whisk the egg whites with 50g of the icing sugar until stiff peaks form.

In a separate bowl, whisk together the remaining icing sugar and the whole eggs until thick and pale. Fold in the ground hazelnuts gently, sift in the flour, then fold in the melted butter. Finally, gently fold in the whisked egg whites.

Divide the mixture evenly between the prepared cake tins. Bake for 12–15 minutes, until golden brown or an inserted skewer comes out

clean. Allow the cakes to cool in their tins for about 10 minutes, then turn out on to wire racks to cool completely.

HAZELNUT MILK CHOCOLATE BUTTERCREAM

125g unsalted butter, at room temperature
250g icing sugar
1 teaspoon vanilla extract
2 tablespoons double cream or whole milk
100g Nutella or other hazelnut chocolate
  spread

To make the buttercream, beat the butter and icing sugar together until smooth. Add the vanilla extract and the cream or milk and beat until combined. Add the Nutella and beat on a low speed until smooth.

CHOCOLATE GANACHE

200g dark chocolate (70% cocoa solids),
  chopped
200ml double cream

Place the chocolate in a heatproof bowl. In a saucepan, heat the cream on a medium heat until almost boiling. Pour it immediately over the chocolate and let it sit for about 2 minutes. Mix gently with a spatula until smooth and the chocolate is fully melted.

ASSEMBLE

whole hazelnuts, toasted, to decorate

To assemble the cake, place one layer of sponge on a cake board or plate and cover the top with some of the buttercream. Place another layer of sponge on top and cover with chocolate ganache. Add the last layer of sponge, then cover the top and sides of the cake with the remaining buttercream. Decorate the top of the cake with the toasted whole hazelnuts.

WALNUT STREUSEL CAKE

The walnut crumb or streusel topping of this cake adds a delicious finishing touch to the vanilla sponge underneath and could be served with cream or ice-cream as an extra treat.

Makes one single layer 20cm cake, serving 10–12

STREUSEL TOPPING

75g unsalted butter, at room temperature
75g soft light brown sugar
90g plain flour
75g walnut halves

Place all the streusel topping ingredients in a bowl. Using your fingertips, rub all the ingredients together until well combined. Cover the bowl and place in the freezer until ready to use.

CAKE

200g self-raising flour
¼ teaspoon salt
150g unsalted butter, at room temperature
180g golden caster sugar
2 large eggs
1½ teaspoons vanilla extract
50ml milk
1 tablespoon vegetable oil

Preheat the oven to 180°C/160°C (fan)/gas mark 4. Grease a deep 20cm cake tin and line with parchment paper.

Sift the flour and salt together and set aside.

Cream the butter and sugar together in another bowl until light and fluffy. Add the eggs one at a time, making sure each one is well incorporated before adding the next. Add the vanilla with the second egg.

Add the flour and salt and beat until just combined. Pour in the milk and oil and beat until smooth.

Pour the mixture into the cake tin and spread the batter out to the sides, making sure it is evenly distributed.

Take the streusel topping out of the freezer and break up any large pieces. Sprinkle the streusel evenly over the top of the cake batter.

Bake for 45–50 minutes, until golden brown and firm on top and an inserted skewer comes out clean.

Allow the cake to cool in its tin for about 10–15 minutes, then turn out on to a wire rack to cool completely. Let it cool fully before cutting.

COOKIES

Here is a big choice of cookies to prepare for Santa's arrival on Christmas Eve, or alternatively to just make and eat together as a family or to take round to friends and family. Some of these are popular sellers in the bakeries already – others we have had fun developing and tasting in our kitchens.

The cookies should all keep well for at least five days in an airtight container or securely wrapped, which makes them a good choice for any baking you want to do in advance.

CHOCOLATE CARAMEL COOKIES

A popular seller in our bakeries already – who can resist the combination of chocolate and caramel! It will be hard to eat just one.

Makes 15 cookies

115g unsalted butter, at room temperature
175g golden caster sugar
1 large egg
½ teaspoon vanilla extract
175g plain flour
½ teaspoon bicarbonate of soda
½ teaspoon salt
50g dark chocolate chips (70% cocoa solids)
125g caramel chocolate chips (we use a brand
   called Callebaut, which you should be able to
   get online)

Preheat the oven to 180°C/160°C (fan)/gas mark 4. Lightly grease 3 baking trays and line with parchment paper.

Cream together the butter and sugar with an electric mixer until light and fluffy. Add the egg and vanilla extract and mix until combined.

Sift in the flour, bicarbonate of soda and salt and beat until they are all mixed in. Fold in the chocolate and caramel chips with a wooden spoon.

Wrap the dough in cling film and allow to rest in the fridge for at least 30 minutes – overnight would even be OK if you wanted to prepare it in advance.

Portion the dough into 15 equal pieces and roll each one into a ball. Place 4–5 rolled balls on each tray, so that there is enough space for the cookies to spread.

Bake for 12–15 minutes, or until the edges start browning but the centre is still slightly soft. Do not allow them to cook until they are all hard.

Leave on the trays for 3–5 minutes, then transfer to a wire rack to cool completely.

TRIPLE CHOCOLATE COOKIES

*Another fantastic combination of chocolates –
who could ask for more in a cookie?*

Makes 25 cookies

200g unsalted butter, at room temperature
250g soft light brown sugar
1 large egg
1 teaspoon vanilla extract
**150g dark chocolate (70% cocoa solids),
  melted**
320g plain flour
1 teaspoon bicarbonate of soda
¼ teaspoon baking powder
150g milk chocolate chips
150g white chocolate chips

Preheat the oven to 180°C/160°C (fan)/gas
mark 4. Line 2 or 3 baking trays with parchment
paper and set aside.

Cream the butter and sugar together in a
bowl until they are light and creamy. Add the
egg and vanilla extract and mix until combined.
Pour in the melted chocolate and mix until
just combined.

Sift in the flour, bicarbonate of soda and
baking powder. Mix until all the ingredients
are combined and resemble soft dough.
Fold in the chocolate chips with a spatula or
wooden spoon.

Wrap the dough in cling film and rest in the
fridge for at least 10–15 minutes.

Portion the dough into 25 equal pieces. Roll
each piece into a ball and flatten to a disc
shape measuring 6cm in diameter and with a thickness
of approximately 1cm. Place a maximum of
5–6 on each tray, allowing enough space for the
cookies to spread.

Bake on the middle and top racks of the oven
for 5 minutes, then turn the trays around and
bake for a further 4 minutes. Remove from the
oven. The cookies will be slightly firm around the
edge and still slightly soft in the middle. Allow
them to cool on the tray before removing.

MINCE PIE COOKIES

Primrose Bakery's amazing manager, Sally, developed these cookies to try to combine our love of cookies with using mincemeat, as it is such a Christmas staple. You can either make your own mincemeat or simply jazz up a shop-bought version, depending on how much time you have. They would be even nicer served with a glass of mulled wine and would make a good petit four to serve if entertaining over Christmas.

Makes 10–20 cookies, depending on their size

HOMEMADE MINCEMEAT
(to be made at least 2 weeks in advance)

2 Bramley apples, cut into small cubes
  with skin on
100g raisins
90g currants
90g dried pitted dates
75g dried cranberries
50g candied mixed peel
90g soft light brown sugar
zest and juice of ½ an orange
zest and juice of ½ a lemon
50g toasted almonds, roughly chopped
½ teaspoon ground allspice
¼ teaspoon ground cloves
¼ teaspoon ground nutmeg
100g shredded suet (beef or vegetarian)
2 tablespoons brandy
2 tablespoons amaretto

Combine all the ingredients in a large bowl except for the brandy and amaretto. Mix well, then cover the bowl with cling film and leave to sit overnight for the flavours to develop.

The next day, preheat the oven to 110°C/90°C (fan)/gas mark ¼. Put the contents of the bowl on a lined baking tray and stir well. Cover with foil and bake for 3 hours, stirring every 30 minutes.

Remove from the oven, take the foil off and allow to cool completely. Stir the mixture occasionally while it is cooling. When it has completely cooled, stir in the brandy and amaretto.

Pack into sterilised glass jars and refrigerate for at least 2 weeks before using.

Note: To sterilise glass jars, preheat the oven to 110°C/90°C (fan)/gas mark ¼. Wash the jars and lids in hot, soapy water and rinse well. Fill a large saucepan with cold water and place the washed jars and lids in the water. Bring the water to a boil over a high heat and boil for 10 minutes. Line a baking tray with a tea towel and place the jars upside down on the tea towel, using metal tongs. Heat the jars and lids in the oven for 15 minutes and allow to cool before using. Do not place cooled mincemeat into hot jars as it may cause the glass to crack.

MINCEMEAT MIX FOR THE COOKIES

140g good-quality mincemeat (homemade or shop bought)
zest of 1 lemon
1 vanilla pod
30g chopped walnuts
30g chopped pecans
100ml amaretto

Put the mincemeat in a bowl and add the lemon zest, vanilla and the chopped walnuts and pecans. Stir everything together.

Slowly add the amaretto until half the mix is covered. Leave to soak for at least 2–3 hours, but preferably overnight if time permits. More amaretto can be added if you like a stronger flavour.

COOKIES

225g unsalted butter, at room temperature
140g caster sugar
1 egg yolk
280g plain flour
a pinch of salt
mincemeat mix (see above)

Preheat the oven to 180°C/160°C (fan)/gas mark 4. Lightly grease a few baking trays and line with parchment paper.

Using an electric mixer, cream together the butter and sugar until light and fluffy. Beat the egg yolk into the mixture. Sift in the flour and salt and beat on a low speed until it is all mixed together.

Now fold in the mincemeat a little at a time until it is all combined. The mixture will be sticky and a little wet.

Wrap half the mixture in cling film and shape it into a log. Twist each end of the cling film and tie a knot so the mix doesn't come out at the end. Leave the dough to rest in the fridge until it has hardened. Repeat the process with the other half of the dough.

Once the dough has hardened, remove the cling film and, using a sharp knife, cut the dough into slices approximately 5mm thick. If you would like a larger cookie, cut thicker slices.

Put the cookie slices on the lined baking trays, making sure there is at least 3cm between them. Leave the cookies on the trays for 15–20 minutes, to allow them to come up to room temperature.

Bake in the oven for 10–12 minutes, or until they are golden brown on the outside but still a little soft in the centre. Leave to cool on a wire rack – but they can also be enjoyed while still warm.

OREO CHOCOLATE CHIP COOKIES

My two daughters, Daisy and Millie, love Oreos in every form, so Daisy decided to make these cookies with Oreos in the middle and they were both very happy with the outcome.

Makes 12 cookies

220g plain flour
½ teaspoon salt
½ teaspoon bicarbonate of soda
120g unsalted butter, at room temperature
75g light brown sugar
110g granulated sugar
1 large egg
½ teaspoon vanilla extract
140g dark chocolate chips
12 Oreo cookies

Preheat the oven to 180°C/160°C (fan)/gas mark 4. Lightly grease 2 or 3 baking trays and line with parchment paper.

Sift the flour, salt and bicarbonate of soda into a bowl and set aside. Cream the butter and sugars together with an electric mixer until light and fluffy.

Beat in the egg and vanilla extract. Add the dry ingredients and beat on a low speed until they are all combined. Fold in the chocolate chips with a spatula or wooden spoon.

Using a large spoon or scoop, divide the cookie dough into even portions. Wrap each Oreo cookie with one portion of the cookie dough mixture and form a ball. Make sure it is not too big.

Wrap the cookie dough balls in cling film and chill in the fridge for at least 15 minutes, to let the dough rest. Put a maximum of 5 cookies on each baking tray and bake for 10–15 minutes, or until they are golden brown.

Allow to cool, or eat while still warm.

SMARTIES COOKIES

Our head chef, Daniel, made these colourful cookies, which would be fun to make with children on a cold winter's day and then eat with a glass of cold milk on the side.

Makes 16 cookies

150g good-quality dark chocolate (70% cocoa solids)
50g unsalted butter, at room temperature
2 large eggs
250g golden caster sugar
1 teaspoon vanilla extract
50g plain flour
¼ teaspoon baking powder
100g good-quality dark chocolate chips
1 family bag of Smarties or a few tubes

Preheat the oven to 180°C/160°C (fan)/gas mark 4. Line a couple of baking trays with parchment paper.

Melt the 150g of dark chocolate and the butter in a suitable bowl in the microwave or in a heatproof bowl over a pan of simmering water, then allow to cool.

In a bowl, beat the eggs, sugar and vanilla until pale and fluffy. Add the melted chocolate and butter and combine well. Sift in the flour and baking powder and mix well, followed by the chocolate chips. The mixture may be quite wet at this stage, so wrap the bowl in cling film and let it rest in the fridge for 1–2 hours to firm up into a dough.

Weigh out or estimate 50g balls of the cookie dough. Place 8 on each tray, making sure you allow space for them to spread. Flatten each cookie slightly and press about 7 Smarties into each one.

Bake for 8 minutes, then rotate the trays and cook for a further 8 minutes. Allow to cool on the trays before serving.

SPICED CHRISTMAS OR LINZER COOKIES

Linzertorte and Linzer cookies, originating from Linz in Austria, are famous and traditional European Christmas pastries. The combination of spices has a very distinctive and delicious smell and taste.

Makes 15 sandwich cookies or 30 thumbprint cookies

200g plain flour
1 teaspoon bicarbonate of soda
¼ teaspoon salt
1 teaspoon ground cinnamon
½ teaspoon ground cloves
1 teaspoon ground nutmeg
125g unsalted butter, at room temperature
180g golden caster sugar
zest of ½ a lemon
zest of ½ an orange
1 large egg
1 teaspoon vanilla extract
raspberry jam (approx. 15 small teaspoons)

Preheat the oven to 180°C/160°C (fan)/gas mark 4. Lightly grease 2 or 3 baking trays and line with parchment paper.

Sift all the dry ingredients (except the caster sugar) together into a bowl and set aside.

Cream the butter, sugar and zests together until light and fluffy. Add the egg and vanilla and beat until combined. Add the sifted dry ingredients and beat on a low speed until the mixture forms a soft dough. Wrap in cling film and rest in the fridge for 15–20 minutes. The dough can now be used to make two variations of cookie.

TO MAKE SANDWICH COOKIES

Place the dough on a flat surface lightly dusted with plain flour. Using a rolling pin, roll the dough out to approximately 3mm in thickness. Using a cookie cutter such as a heart, star or circle, cut out an even number of cookies. On every second cookie, using a smaller cookie cutter of the same shape, cut out a piece from the middle.

Put them carefully on to the lined baking trays, ensuring they are at least 2cm apart. Bake until the edges turn golden brown or they are firm to touch in the middle. This will be approximately 8–10 minutes. Let the cookies cool completely before sandwiching them together with raspberry jam.

TO MAKE THUMBPRINT COOKIES

Take small pieces of the dough and roll them into equal balls. Place the dough balls about 5cm apart on the prepared baking trays.

Using the tip of your thumb, push down on each dough ball and make a deep indent. Do not push too far down, as there should be dough on the bottom of the cookies. Using a small dessert spoon, carefully and neatly place a small amount of raspberry jam into each indent. Be sure not to have the jam spilling over the edge. Bake until the edges turn golden brown or they are slightly firm to touch. This should take about 12–15 minutes.

FRESH MINT SHORTBREAD BISCUITS

Shortbread is another Christmas necessity, and our chef Laurel decided to make it slightly different by adding fresh mint. You could also substitute the mint with orange zest or vanilla, for example. We have also made these into a chequerboard design, to add to the Christmas feel with pink/red and white.

Makes 15 cookies

275g plain flour
a pinch of salt
100g icing sugar
195g unsalted butter, at room temperature
15–20 fresh mint leaves, roughly chopped
a few drops of red food colouring

Preheat the oven to 180°C/160°C (fan)/gas mark 4.

Lightly grease 2 or 3 baking trays and line with parchment paper.

Sift the flour, salt and icing sugar into a bowl. Add the butter and mint leaves and mix until just combined and a dough has formed.

Wrap half the dough in cling film and shape it into a square block. Add a few drops of red food colouring to the other half of the dough and mix until it is evenly coloured – it will be a pinkish red. Wrap it in cling film and shape it into a similar square block. Rest both doughs in the fridge for 15–20 minutes.

Cut each square of dough in half and stack them alternately on top of each other, pressing down lightly on each layer to get them to stick together. Slice the new block into square cookie shapes, which should have a chequered appearance.

Bake for 8–12 minutes, or until the biscuits are firm to touch and a very light golden brown. Cool on a wire rack.

BRANDY SNAPS

This is one of my favourite desserts. We have added some brandy to give it an added edge, although it is not a necessity. A simple but fantastic festive dessert.

Makes 12

55g plain flour
½ teaspoon ground ginger
a pinch of salt
60g unsalted butter
50g golden syrup
50g golden caster sugar
2 tablespoons brandy

Preheat the oven to 180°C/160°C (fan)/gas mark 4. Lightly grease 2 baking trays and line with parchment paper.

Sift the flour, ginger and salt into a bowl and make a well in the centre. Set aside.

Put the butter, syrup and sugar into a pan and gently melt over a low heat until the sugar has dissolved, stirring constantly with a wooden spoon. Bring the mixture to the boil for 1 minute, then pour into the well in the flour mixture. Stir quickly until everything is just combined. Stir in the brandy.

Spoon ½ a tablespoon of mixture at a time on to the baking tray, with a maximum of 6 per tray. Allow space for them to spread while cooking.

Bake for 8–10 minutes, or until they are golden and lacy in appearance. Do not overcook them. Remove from the oven and allow to cool for

1–2 minutes, then lift up the brandy snaps one at a time with a palette knife and wrap them around the handle of a lightly greased wooden spoon.

Press the join lightly to seal. Once each brandy snap is cool enough to hold its shape, slide it off the handle and allow to cool completely before filling.

If any of the brandy snaps cool before you are able to roll them, put them back into the oven for a few seconds so they become soft and pliable, again.

The unfilled brandy snaps can be kept for up to 5 days in an airtight container. This makes them a great dessert to prepare in advance.

BRANDY CREAM FILLING

150ml double or whipping cream
25g icing sugar
1 tablespoon brandy (or to taste)

Pour the cream into a clean bowl. Sift the icing sugar into the cream and add the brandy. Whisk the cream until it forms medium/stiff peaks. Ideally using a piping bag with a star nozzle, pipe the cream into the cooled brandy snaps before serving. If you don't have a piping bag, you can carefully fill the brandy snaps using a small teaspoon.

You can keep any uneaten filled brandy snaps in the fridge for a day or so, but the brandy snap itself will start to go soft, so they are best eaten soon after they are prepared.

EARL GREY, ALMOND AND WHITE CHOCOLATE BISCOTTI

These would make a good after-dinner biscuit to serve with coffee, or a treat with a cup of tea after a long day.

Makes 15 cookies

150g plain flour
½ teaspoon baking powder
a pinch of salt
2 tablespoons loose-leaf Earl Grey tea
  (or tea leaves from Earl Grey tea bags)
90g unsalted butter, at room temperature
115g golden caster sugar
1 large egg
¼ teaspoon almond extract
50g white chocolate, melted, to drizzle on top

Preheat the oven to 180°C/160°C (fan)/gas mark 4. Lightly grease a baking tray and line with parchment paper.

Sift the flour and baking powder together into a bowl. Add the Earl Grey tea leaves and stir to combine. Set aside.

Cream the butter and sugar together in another bowl until light and fluffy. Add the egg and almond extract and beat until well combined. Add the flour and tea mixture and mix until just combined.

Shape the dough into a log about 5–6cm wide and place it on the lined baking tray. Bake in the oven for 30–35 minutes, by which time it should be a light golden brown colour.

Remove from the oven and cool for 15–20 minutes. Do not turn the oven off. Place the log on a cutting board and, using a serrated knife, cut it on the diagonal into 1cm-thick slices. Place the slices back on the baking tray and put the tray into the oven. Bake for 10 minutes, then turn the biscotti over and bake for a further 10–15 minutes, until they are golden brown.

Transfer the biscotti on to a wire rack to cool completely.

Once cooled, drizzle each biscotti with melted white chocolate in a criss-cross pattern.

GINGER SPARKLE COOKIES

These cookies really do sparkle! So they would work fantastically well at Christmas, to eat at teatime round the Christmas tree or perhaps while wrapping presents.

Makes 15–20 cookies

280g plain flour
2½ teaspoons ground ginger
¾ teaspoon ground cinnamon
½ teaspoon ground cloves
1 teaspoon bicarbonate of soda
¼ teaspoon salt
180g unsalted butter, at room temperature
225g golden caster sugar
60g molasses sugar or dark brown sugar
1 large egg
1 tablespoon water
80g coarse or granulated sugar

Preheat the oven to 180°C/160°C (fan)/gas mark 4. Lightly grease a couple of baking trays and line with parchment paper.

Sift the flours, spices, bicarbonate of soda and salt into a bowl and set aside.

In a separate bowl, cream the butter and sugars until light and fluffy. Add the egg and beat until well combined. On a low speed, add all the sifted dry ingredients and mix until the dough just comes together. Add the water and mix to combine. Wrap the dough in cling film and form into a long sausage shape. Let it rest in the fridge for 30 minutes.

Put the coarse or granulated sugar into a bowl. Cut the dough into 15–20 evenly sized pieces then roll each one into a ball. Roll each dough ball in the bowl of sugar, then place them evenly spaced out on the trays. The dough balls should be at least 3cm apart to allow room for the cookies to spread when baking.

Bake for 15–18 minutes, until the edges of the cookies are slightly firm and the centre is still a little soft. Let them cool on the trays for about 5 minutes before removing.

These are delicious served warm. Keep any spare ones in an airtight container.

RASPBERRY AND PISTACHIO THUMBPRINT COOKIES

Another lovely mixture of flavours and colours, these cookies are so named as you really do make a thumbprint indentation into each one to fill with the jam.

Makes 12 cookies

120g unsalted butter, at room temperature
65g golden caster sugar
1 large egg, separated
a pinch of salt
½ teaspoon vanilla extract
150g plain flour
100g finely chopped unsalted pistachios
**raspberry jam, for filling (about 12 small
   teaspoons)**

Preheat the oven to 180°C/160°C (fan)/gas mark 4. Lightly grease a baking tray and line with parchment paper.

In a bowl, beat the butter, sugar, egg yolk, salt and vanilla together until light and fluffy. Sift in the flour and combine on a low speed. Rest the dough in the fridge for 30–60 minutes.

Shape the dough into 12 small balls and roll each one first in the egg white, then in the chopped pistachios. Place on a baking tray and make a thumbprint in each one. Make sure there is at least a 2–3cm space between the cookies. Bake them for 5 minutes, then remove from the oven.

Press the thumbprint hole again and fill it with raspberry jam. Be careful not to overfill. Bake for another 10–12 minutes, until they are a light golden brown and firm to touch.

Let the cookies cool on the tray for about 5 minutes before removing. Allow to cool before eating, as the jam will be very hot and you could burn your mouth. Keep any uneaten ones in an airtight container.

SPECULOOS BISCUIT TREE DECORATIONS

These traditional northern European spiced shortbread biscuits were usually served around the time of St Nicholas' feast (early December) and at Christmas, but are now eaten year round. Our assistant manager, Rachel, is rightly obsessed with speculoos and was determined to introduce them to the bakery.

Makes 10–15 biscuits

220g plain flour
2 teaspoons ground cinnamon
1 teaspoon ground ginger
1 teaspoon ground nutmeg
1 teaspoon cloves
1 teaspoon baking powder
½ teaspoon salt
100g soft brown sugar
1 tablespoon milk
150g butter, at room temperature
10–15 pieces of ribbon or string (35cm in length) – optional if wanting to make tree decorations

Preheat the oven to 180°C/160°C (fan)/gas mark 4. Line a baking tray with parchment paper.

Sift the flour, spices, baking powder and salt into a bowl. Add the brown sugar and break up any lumps with your hands. Add the milk and butter, then use your hands to bring the mixture together as a dough. Rest the dough in the fridge for 30 minutes.

Turn the dough out on to a lightly floured work surface and roll out to a 5mm thickness. A pattern can be imprinted on to the dough before cutting to create a lovely surface when the biscuits are baked. This can be done by using a textured rolling pin to roll over the dough just before cutting out the shapes. The textured rolling pin should only be used for the final roll. The dough should be approximately 7–8mm in thickness before you use the textured rolling pin.

Cut out the biscuits using a circular cutter or any other shape desired. If you want to hang them on the tree once they are made, use a piping tip nozzle that has a 3–4mm opening, and cut out a hole at one end of each biscuit. These holes will be used to thread ribbon through once baked and cooled.

Place the biscuits on the lined baking tray with at least a 2–3cm gap between them. Bake for 15–18 minutes, or until golden brown and firm to touch. Set aside to cool on a wire rack.

Thread the pre-cut ribbons or strings through the holes in the biscuits and tie the ends together. Hang the biscuits on your Christmas tree to decorate. They can be made in advance and kept for up to a week in an airtight container.

SPECULOOS COOKIE BUTTER

This is an added extra you can make using the speculoos cookies from the previous recipe. Use it for spreading on toast or, if you are like our Rachel, just eat it straight from the jar!

Makes one 400g jar

80g unsalted butter
250g speculoos cookies (1 batch of biscuits, see page 142)
1½ tablespoons ground cinnamon
¼ teaspoon ground nutmeg
a pinch of ground cloves
a pinch of ground ginger
1 teaspoon vanilla extract
1 tablespoon soft brown sugar
4 tablespoons corn oil (any flavourless oil will do)
60g good-quality white chocolate, melted

Melt the butter in a small pan over a high heat, until golden brown. Set aside to cool slightly.

Toss the speculoos biscuits into a food processor and process on full power until they are finely crushed. Turn the processor off and scrape down the sides if necessary. Add all the spices, the vanilla and brown sugar and process until combined. Pour in the melted butter and process on high. Your mixture will turn from a paste into a thick/stubborn paste. Turn the processor off and scrape down the sides. Add the oil a tablespoon at a time through the feed tube with the food processor on high power. You may add more oil if you desire a runnier cookie butter. Remember that it will firm up as it cools.

When you've reached the desired consistency, pour in the melted white chocolate and process until just combined.

Pour your cookie butter into a sterilised glass jar with a screw top lid. Stir before using, then allow to set. It will keep well in a cool dark place for up to 5 days.

GINGERBREAD SAUSAGE DOGS

Any Primrose Bakery fan will know how important sausage dogs in all shapes and forms are to us, mostly because of Charlie the dachshund, the bakery mascot. He loves nothing more than a trip to the bakery, where Sally feeds him croissants. These gingerbread biscuits can be made in any shape, however, and can be eaten, given as presents or hung on the tree as decorations.

Makes 15–20 biscuits

75g soft dark brown sugar
50g golden syrup
25g black treacle or molasses
1 teaspoon ground cinnamon
1 teaspoon ground ginger
a pinch of ground cloves
a pinch of ground nutmeg
rind of ½ an orange, grated
95g unsalted butter
225g plain flour
½ teaspoon bicarbonate of soda

You will need a sausage dog or other shape biscuit cutter.

Preheat the oven to 180°C/160°C (fan)/gas mark 4. Line a couple of baking trays with parchment paper.

Put the brown sugar, golden syrup, black treacle, spices and grated orange rind into a pan and heat until the sugar is dissolved. This should take about 3–5 minutes over a high heat.

Remove the pan from the heat and stir in the butter until it is completely melted. Stir in the flour and bicarbonate of soda and a soft dough should form. Wrap this in cling film and refrigerate for at least 1 hour, though you can leave it overnight.

Once you are ready to cook the biscuits, roll the dough out on a large, flat, floured work surface to a thickness of about 2mm. Cut out the sausage dogs (or whatever shape you would like) carefully with the biscuit cutter and place each one on the baking tray, leaving a little space between them.

Bake in the oven for 8–10 minutes. To tell if they are cooked, feel the centre of the biscuit, which should feel stiff but not hard. The edges must not be too dark, otherwise the resulting biscuit will be brittle and bitter to taste.

Allow the gingerbread to cool fully before icing. You can use royal or water icing to ice these sausage dogs. Alternatively we find the tubes of Silver Spoon designer icing very good for this kind of decorating – they are readily available in supermarkets and come in a good variety of colours.

Allow the icing to set a little before serving. These gingerbread sausage dogs also make great presents – you can wrap each one individually in a cellophane bag and tie with a ribbon. Alternatively you can make a hole in the top of each one before baking, and turn them into Christmas tree or other hanging decorations by putting a small piece of ribbon through the hole once they have cooled and been decorated.

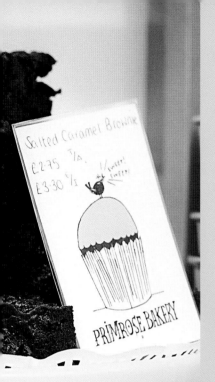

LOAVES AND SLICES

After cupcakes, the next most popular things we sell in our shops are probably our loaves and slices – the lemon drizzle loaf (the recipe for which you will find in the second book, *The Primrose Bakery Book*) has quite possibly been on sale every day since we opened the shop, and now some of the loaves and slices you find in this chapter are beginning to prove just as popular.

Any of these loaves or slices should keep well in an airtight container for a good few days and, like the cookies, are good added extras or standbys for those last-minute teas and get-togethers that seem to happen so much leading up to Christmas.

STICKY TOFFEE LOAF

This rich, sticky loaf is so good that it is hard to eat only one slice. It would be ideal served with a cup of coffee or tea – and to really spoil yourself you could pour some cream over it or serve it with vanilla ice-cream.

Makes one 900g loaf, serving 8–10

225g dried pitted dates, roughly chopped
300ml cold water
1 teaspoon bicarbonate of soda
juice of ½ a lemon
115g unsalted butter, at room temperature
170g light brown sugar
2 large eggs
1 teaspoon vanilla extract
170g self-raising flour

Preheat the oven to 180°C/160°C (fan)/gas mark 4. Lightly grease a 900g loaf tin and line it with parchment paper or a loaf tin liner.

Put the chopped dates and water into a pan and boil until no water remains. Immediately after removing from the heat, add the bicarbonate of soda and lemon juice and stir to combine thoroughly.

While the dates are cooking, cream the butter and sugar together until light and fluffy. Add the eggs one at a time, making sure the first is thoroughly mixed in before adding the next. Add the vanilla with the second egg. Beat until combined. Sift in the flour and mix until just combined.

Add the warm date mixture to the batter and fold in with a spatula to combine. Pour the batter into the loaf tin and place it on the middle rack of the oven. Bake for 40–45 minutes, or until an inserted skewer comes out clean. Allow the loaf to cool before finishing with the sauce and brittle as directed below.

Note: The loaf browns very quickly, so you may need to cover it with foil when it becomes dark brown towards the end of the cooking time to stop the top from burning.

PECAN BRITTLE
(for decoration)

120g granulated sugar
50g pecans, roughly chopped

Cut two sheets of parchment paper. Place one sheet on top of a surface that can withstand high heat and keep the other close by. Place a rolling pin next to the parchment paper.

Put the sugar into a heavy-based pan and heat on a medium heat until it dissolves. Do not stir the sugar, just swirl it in the pan to move it around. Heat until it is amber/golden brown in colour, then turn the heat off immediately. Do not leave it for too long on the heat as the sugar will burn.

Immediately add the chopped pecans to the caramel and swirl the pan to coat. Then pour all the contents of the pan at once on to the parchment paper.

Place the second sheet of parchment paper directly on top of the mixture. Be careful when handling this mixture, as it is very hot and can burn.

Use the rolling pin to quickly roll out the mixture to a thin sheet.

Set aside to cool completely.

SALTED CARAMEL SAUCE

110g granulated sugar
3 tablespoons water
125ml double cream
1 teaspoon fleur de sel

Note: This is a very hot liquid, so please be careful when making it.

Put the sugar and water into a clean medium pan and place it over a medium heat on the hob. Do not stir the mixture, as this will cause the sugar syrup to crystallise. Swirl the pan occasionally and gently until all the sugar has dissolved. Then turn the heat up to high and let the syrup boil.

While the sugar syrup is boiling, pour the cream into another pan and add the fleur de sel. Heat gently over a medium heat until it is warmish, but do not boil.

Once the sugar syrup turns a golden colour remove from it from heat and immediately add a small portion (say 1–2 tablespoons) of the warm cream. Stir quickly with a wooden spoon to prevent it sticking to the bottom of the pan. Be careful when adding the cream, as it will bubble up and rise very quickly and let off a lot of hot steam and may splutter. Add the remainder of the cream in small amounts. Keep stirring while the cream is being added.

Pour the sauce into a bowl and set it aside to cool.

ASSEMBLE

To assemble, use a skewer to poke holes all over the loaf, then brush some of the salted caramel sauce over the top. Place a single row of small pieces of pecan brittle lengthways along the loaf.

The remaining salted caramel sauce can be served with the cake.

NATURAL RED VELVET LOAF ✳

The craze for red velvet cakes and cupcakes doesn't seem to be waning, so we made a loaf version of our popular natural red velvet cupcakes. The colours of this loaf are in fact quite Christmassy. One word of caution: our version of red velvet sponge does have a more earthy, natural taste than classic red velvet cake, as we felt very strongly about not using a huge quantity of red food colouring.

Makes one 900g loaf, serving 8–10

BEETROOT PURÉE

1 raw beetroot (approx. 140g)
35g frozen raspberries
½ tablespoon apple cider vinegar
½ tablespoon cold water

First make the beetroot purée. Peel the beetroot and cut into cubes. Place the beetroot, raspberries, apple cider vinegar and water in a food processor and process for 5 minutes, scraping down the sides every couple of minutes. Place in a bowl and set aside.

CAKE

230g self-raising flour
a pinch of salt
40g dark chocolate (70% cocoa solids)
70g unsalted butter, at room temperature
185g golden caster sugar
2 large eggs
1½ teaspoons vanilla extract
75ml buttermilk (or 70ml milk and juice of ½ a lemon)
1½ teaspoons natural red food colouring
140g beetroot purée

Preheat the oven to 180°C/160°C (fan)/gas mark 4. Lightly grease a loaf tin with and line with parchment paper or a loaf tin liner.

Sift the flour and salt into a bowl and set aside. Melt the chocolate in a suitable bowl in a microwave or in a heatproof bowl over a pan of simmering water on the hob. Keep warm and set aside.

Put the butter, sugar, eggs and vanilla in a bowl and beat on a medium/high speed for 4–5 minutes, until pale, light and fluffy.

Pour in the melted chocolate and beat on a low speed until combined. Add the flour and salt and beat on a low speed until just combined. Pour in the buttermilk and the natural red food colouring and beat on a low speed until well combined.

Add the beetroot purée to the mixture and fold in gently with a spatula.

Pour the batter into the lined loaf tin and bake for 35–40 minutes, or until an inserted skewer comes out clean. Allow to cool completely.

CREAM CHEESE ICING

40g unsalted butter, at room temperature
95g cream cheese
juice of ¼ of a lemon
280g icing sugar, sifted

Place the butter, cream cheese, lemon juice and half the icing sugar in a bowl and beat on a low speed until all the ingredients are combined. Add the remaining icing sugar and beat on a low speed until everything is combined. Turn the beater on to high speed and beat the icing for 3–4 minutes, or until it is white and fluffy.

ASSEMBLE

red ball sprinkles (optional)

Ice the surface of the loaf with the cream cheese icing. If you like, sprinkle with red ball sprinkles.

If you have any spare icing, keep it in the fridge in an airtight container.

SPICED FRUIT LOAF

This fruit and nut loaf would be good served at breakfast on Christmas morning or at teatime on Christmas Eve. You could even toast some slices and butter them.

Makes one 900g loaf, serving 8–10

150g unsalted butter, at room temperature
175g light brown sugar
2 large eggs
250g self-raising flour
1 teaspoon baking powder
juice of 1 orange
2 teaspoons mixed spice
1 teaspoon ground cinnamon
100g raisins
50g dried cherries
50g dried cranberries
50g chopped walnuts

Preheat the oven to 180°C/160°C (fan)/gas mark 4. Lightly grease a loaf tin and line with parchment paper or a loaf tin liner.

In a bowl, cream together the butter and sugar until pale and fluffy. Add the eggs one at a time, ensuring they are thoroughly mixed in. Sift in the flour, baking powder and spices, and mix until well combined. Add the orange juice and beat again until smooth. Finally, fold in the dried fruit and chopped walnuts.

Put the batter into the lined loaf tin and bake in the oven for 45–60 minutes. Allow to cool slightly before serving.

ROCKY ROAD SLICE

This is a very popular slice in the bakery, and certain staff are known to watch out for any off-cuts when we are making it and suddenly appear extra helpful in the kitchen! Pink marshmallows would look pretty in these, against the dark chocolate.

Makes one 33 x 23cm tray bake, serving 15

188g unsalted butter
450g dark chocolate (70% cocoa solids)
75g golden syrup
300g Rich Tea biscuits
150g dried cranberries
150g dried sour cherries
150g marshmallows, quartered, plus extra
  marshmallows for the top
50g white chocolate, melted

Lightly grease a 33 x 23cm baking tin and line with parchment paper.

Put the butter, dark chocolate and golden syrup into a microwaveable bowl or a pan. Heat carefully in the microwave or on the hob until it is all melted, then set aside.

In a separate large bowl, crush the Rich Tea biscuits into chunks with the end of a rolling pin or wooden spoon. Add the dried fruit and quartered marshmallows and mix together.

Pour the melted chocolate mixture on top of the crushed biscuits and stir until all the pieces are coated.

Pour the mixture into the lined baking tin, pressing it into the sides to make it even and slightly compact. Randomly place the extra marshmallows on top.

Place the tin in the fridge for 15–20 minutes, to set the chocolate, then drizzle the melted white chocolate over the top to form a criss-cross pattern.

Put the tin back into the fridge for another 15 minutes, or until the white chocolate sets. Cut into squares or any shape desired before serving.

SALTED CARAMEL BROWNIES

The first of a few of our brownie recipes, this one with our beloved salted caramel which we never tire of and hopefully nor will you.

Makes one 33 x 23cm tray bake, serving 15

300g unsalted butter
120g dark chocolate (70% cocoa solids)
250g caramel chocolate
250g golden caster sugar
40g cocoa
150g plain flour
¼ teaspoon baking powder
3 large eggs
200g salted caramel sauce (see page 152)
fleur de sel, for sprinkling

Preheat the oven to 180°C/160°C (fan)/gas mark 4. Lightly grease a 33 x 23cm baking tin and line with parchment paper.

Place the butter in a microwaveable bowl and melt in the microwave or heat gently in a pan on the hob until it is completely melted. Set aside to cool slightly.

Break the dark and caramel chocolate into chunks. Put the sugar, cocoa, flour, baking powder and chocolates into a large bowl. Stir with a wooden spoon to combine the ingredients. Make a well in the centre.

Pour the melted butter into the dry ingredients and stir with the wooden spoon until well combined. Add the eggs and stir to combine.

Pour the mixture into the lined tin and spread out evenly. Dollop the caramel sauce over the surface of the mixture. Use a skewer to swirl it in. Do not mix it in completely, just try to create a marble effect on the surface.

Sprinkle a little fleur de sel over the top of the brownie.

Place on the middle rack of the oven and bake for 30–35 minutes, or until an inserted skewer comes out clean. The brownie should still be fairly soft to the touch. Allow to cool in the tin, then transfer to a board and cut into the desired number of pieces.

CHEESECAKE BROWNIE

The combination of cheesecake and brownie seems to work well together, and would make a great dessert – or even a cute petit four if cut up into tiny pieces and served at a party.

Makes one 33 x 23cm tray bake, serving 15

CHOCOLATE BROWNIE

200g dark chocolate (70% cocoa solids)
175g unsalted butter, cut into cubes
325g golden caster sugar
3 large eggs
130g plain flour

Preheat the oven to 180°C/160°C (fan)/gas mark 4. Lightly grease a 33 x 23cm baking tin and line with parchment paper.

Place the chocolate and butter in a medium to large microwaveable/heatproof bowl and heat in a microwave or over a pan of simmering water until melted. Stir to combine. Add the sugar and eggs and combine thoroughly.

Sift the plain flour on top of the chocolate mixture and fold in with a spatula.

Pour the mixture into the lined baking tin and spread it out evenly. Set aside while you prepare the cheesecake.

CHEESECAKE

400g cream cheese, softened
150g icing sugar, sifted
2 large eggs
½ teaspoon vanilla extract

In a separate bowl, beat the cream cheese and icing sugar together until smooth.

Add the eggs one at a time, making sure the first one is well mixed in before adding the next. Add the vanilla with the second egg.

ASSEMBLE

Place large dollops of the cheesecake mixture randomly all over the brownie mixture in the baking tin. Using a skewer, swirl the cheesecake into the brownie to create a marble effect.

Place on the middle rack of the oven and bake for 25–30 minutes, until it is firm in the middle and an inserted skewer comes out clean. Leave to cool completely before cutting and serving.

FLORENTINE BLONDIE

The fruit and nuts that top this particularly seasonal slice make it slightly less sweet than normal, but just as delicious.

Makes one 33 x 23cm tray bake, serving 15

250g unsalted butter, cut into cubes
180g golden caster sugar
200g plain flour
½ teaspoon baking powder
160g white chocolate chips, or white chocolate broken into small pieces
100g dried cranberries
100g dried sour cherries
60g maraschino cherries, roughly chopped
2 large eggs
1 teaspoon vanilla extract
flaked almonds, to sprinkle on top (optional)

Preheat the oven to 180°C/160°C (fan)/gas mark 4. Lightly grease a 33 x 23cm baking tin and line with parchment paper.

Put the butter into a microwaveable bowl and heat in the microwave until it is melted, or melt gently in a pan on the hob. Set aside to cool.

Put the sugar, flour, baking powder, white chocolate, cranberries and all the cherries into a large bowl. Mix together with a wooden spoon and make a well in the centre. Pour the melted butter into the centre of the well and stir until combined.

Add the eggs and vanilla and continue stirring until thoroughly combined. Pour the batter into the lined tin and spread it out evenly with a spatula. Sprinkle the top with flaked almonds.

Bake on the middle rack of the oven for 20–25 minutes, until light golden brown or until an inserted skewer comes out clean. Allow to cool completely, then cut into the desired number of pieces.

ORANGE MARMALADE SLICE

There are so many amazing marmalades available now to buy – choose your favourite to use in this recipe and the lovely orange citrus smell will fill the whole kitchen while you are baking.

Makes one 33 x 23cm tray bake, serving 15

SLICE

300g unsalted butter, at room temperature
230g soft light brown sugar
3 large eggs
1½ teaspoons vanilla extract
170g plain flour
225g self-raising flour
125ml orange juice
180g fine-cut marmalade
8 oranges, peeled and segmented

Preheat the oven to 180°C/160°C (fan)/gas mark 4. Lightly grease a 33 x 23cm baking tin and line with parchment paper.

Cream the butter and sugar until light and fluffy. Add the eggs one at a time, ensuring each one is well incorporated before adding the next. Add the vanilla with the last egg.

Sift in the plain and self-raising flours and beat on a low speed until just combined. Pour in the orange juice and marmalade and beat until smooth.

Pour the mixture into the lined baking tin and spread it out evenly. Arrange the segmented oranges in 3 columns lengthways down the tin.

Bake on the middle rack of the oven for 35–40 minutes, until golden brown or an inserted skewer comes out clean. Leave the slice in the tin to cool for 10 minutes, then place on a wire rack to cool while you make the glaze.

MARMALADE GLAZE

75g fine-cut marmalade
50ml orange juice

For the marmalade glaze, put the marmalade and orange juice into a small pan and bring to the boil. Once boiling, turn the heat down to a simmer and cook for a further 3–5 minutes or until it thickens. Remove from the heat and set aside to cool slightly.

ASSEMBLE

Brush the warm glaze generously over the top of the slice to give it a shine, then cut and serve once fully cooled.

CHERRY RIPE SLICE

In remembrance of our Australian links and also to please our many Australian members of staff past and present, this slice is our version of the famous chocolate bar that is actually Australia's oldest, dating back to 1924. Its colours and flavours are also very Christmassy, so it fits perfectly here.

Makes one 33 x 23cm tray bake, serving 15

BASE

210g plain flour
50g cocoa powder
135g unsalted butter, at room temperature
150g golden caster sugar
1 large egg
50ml milk

Preheat the oven to 180°C/160°C (fan)/gas mark 4. Lightly grease a 33 x 23cm baking tin and line with parchment paper.

Sift the flour and cocoa into a bowl and set aside. Cream the butter and sugar together in another bowl until light and fluffy. Add the egg and beat until thoroughly combined.

Add the flour and cocoa and mix until just combined. Pour in the milk and beat until smooth. Spoon the mixture into the prepared tin and spread out evenly.

Bake for 15–18 minutes, until it is firm to touch. Remove and let it cool while you prepare the topping. Leave the oven on.

TOPPING

125g unsalted butter, at room temperature
200g golden caster sugar
2 large eggs
1 teaspoon vanilla extract
90g self-raising flour
200g desiccated coconut
2 tablespoons milk
3 tablespoons maraschino cherry syrup (from the jar of cherries – see below)
240g glacé cherries, roughly chopped
170g maraschino cherries, roughly chopped
50g dark chocolate (70% cocoa solids), melted, for drizzling on top

To make the topping, cream the butter and sugar together until light and fluffy. Add the eggs one at a time, ensuring that the first one is well mixed in before adding the next. Add the vanilla with the second egg.

Add the flour and desiccated coconut and mix. Pour in the milk and cherry syrup and mix. Add all the chopped cherries and fold in with a spatula.

Pour the mixture on to the base and spread out evenly. Bake for 30–35 minutes, until it is firm to the touch and starting to go light golden brown. If a skewer comes out clean when inserted, then it is cooked. Once cooled completely, drizzle the melted dark chocolate over the top of the slice in a criss-cross pattern. Cut into the desired shape once the chocolate has set.

PUMPKIN SLICE

This spicy and slightly alcoholic pumpkin slice would actually make a great dessert, served with some whipped or double cream or vanilla ice-cream on the side.

Makes one 33 x 23cm tray bake, serving 15

BASE

140g soft light brown sugar
100g rolled oats
120g plain flour
150g unsalted butter, chilled

Preheat the oven to 180°C/160°C (fan)/gas mark 4. Lightly grease a 33 x 23cm baking tin and line with parchment paper.

To make the base, place the sugar, oats and flour in a bowl and stir to combine. Add the butter and rub into the dry ingredients with your fingertips until the mixture resembles crumbs.

Press the mixture evenly into the baking tin and bake for 15–20 minutes, or until golden brown. Set aside to cool slightly. Leave the oven on while you prepare the topping.

TOPPING

425 pumpkin purée (Libby's canned purée is very good)
2 large eggs
110g golden caster sugar
30g self-raising flour
1 teaspoon ground nutmeg
½ teaspoon ground cinnamon
¼ teaspoon ground cloves
½ teaspoon ground ginger
½ teaspoon salt
50ml dark rum
1 teaspoon vanilla extract
a handful of flaked almonds

For the topping, put all ingredients (except the almonds) in a large bowl and beat until smooth and thoroughly combined.

ASSEMBLE

Pour the pumpkin mixture on top of the cooked base, spreading it out evenly, and sprinkle with the flaked almonds.

Bake for 20–25 minutes, until firm to touch and the almonds are a light golden brown.

Cool completely before cutting and serving.

PISTACHIO AND RASPBERRY LOAF

This loaf would be nice served while still warm, perhaps for breakfast at a weekend or when everyone has time to enjoy it more during their time off work or school between Christmas and the New Year.

Makes one 900g loaf, serving 8-10

LOAF

250g unsalted butter, at room temperature
150g golden caster sugar
135g soft brown sugar
5 large eggs
100g ground pistachios
100g ground almonds
80g plain flour
75g raspberry jam

Preheat the oven to 180°C/160°C (fan)/gas mark 4. Lightly grease a 900g loaf tin and line with parchment paper or a loaf tin liner.

Beat the butter and sugars together with an electric mixer until light and fluffy. Beat in the eggs one at a time, ensuring each one is well combined before adding the next.

Fold in the ground nuts and flour with a spatula.

Place half the batter in the prepared tin, then spread the raspberry jam over that layer and top with the remaining batter.

Bake in the oven for 45–60 minutes, until the loaf is golden brown. When baking there will be a lot of oil from the nuts bubbling around the loaf. The centre must be firm and spring back when touched before you remove it from the oven. If it starts to brown too quickly, cover it with tin foil for the remainder of the cooking time.

Cool for 15–20 minutes then remove from the tin.

GLAZE

120g raspberry jam
2 teaspoons water

To make the glaze, gently heat the raspberry jam and water in a pan on the hob until it is a smooth, syrup-like liquid.

ASSEMBLE

30g pistachios, chopped

Brush the top of the loaf with the warm glaze. Add the chopped pistachios to any remaining raspberry glaze and spoon this mixture down the middle of the loaf for a decorative touch.

PIES AND TARTS

These are a newer edition to Primrose Bakery and are more like desserts than cakes, but they are just as delicious and a great option for any festive meal alongside the traditional mince pies and Christmas cake. They are all fairly rich, but are hard to resist and proper comfort food on those dark winter evenings of which we seem to have so many.

These recipes are a bit more challenging but are well worth the effort – and they are a real achievement and delight to look at when they are placed on the table.

CHRISTMAS TRIFLE WITH CARAMELISED PEACHES

A trifle is a classic Christmas dessert. Our amazing former business manager, Faye, makes this one every year at Christmas, and at other times of the year if given the chance.

Serves 12–15

VICTORIA SPONGE
(makes one 500g sponge)

115g golden caster sugar
½ teaspoon baking powder
105g self-raising flour
12g cornflour
115g unsalted butter, at room temperature
2 large eggs
½ teaspoon vanilla extract
1½ tablespoons semi-skimmed milk

To make the sponge, preheat the oven to 180°C/160°C (fan)/gas mark 4. Grease a 20cm sandwich tin.

Put the sugar, baking powder, flour and cornflour into a food processor and blend until evenly combined. Add the remaining ingredients and process briefly until all is combined. Don't be tempted to leave the processor on and walk away from it, as the batter will quickly overmix and the resulting cake will have a heavy texture.

Pour the batter into the prepared tin and bake in the oven for about 25 minutes, until raised, golden brown and an inserted skewer comes out clean. Leave in the tin for about 10 minutes, then turn out on to a wire rack to cool.

Allow the sponge to cool completely before using in the trifle.

CARAMELISED PEACHES

1 tablespoon unsalted butter
2 medium-sized peaches, cored and cut into
  wedges (approx. 1cm in thickness)
2 tablespoons muscovado sugar (dark brown
  sugar will be fine as a substitute)

To make the caramelised peaches, heat the
butter in a non-stick pan on the hob. Once it is
bubbling, add the peaches and cook for several
minutes, stirring occasionally so they don't stick
to the pan. Add the sugar and cook on a low
heat (approx. 7 minutes), simmering and stirring,
until the peaches look golden and caramelised.
Test with a skewer to check they are cooked
through. Set aside to cool.

ASSEMBLE

300ml double cream
rind of 1 orange
juice of 2 oranges
2 tablespoons sherry (optional)
275g good-quality raspberry jam
300ml good-quality vanilla custard
300g fresh raspberries
60g good-quality chocolate shavings

To assemble the trifle, divide the sponge into
four equal sections (each section will make one
layer). Cut the sponge into strips approximately
2cm in width.

Whisk the cream until it forms soft peaks. Add
the orange rind and delicately fold it through the
cream. Be careful not to overbeat the mixture.
You want a soft, silky, runny texture.

Combine the fresh orange juice and sherry.

Line a 26cm glass serving bowl with an even
layer of sponge, then sprinkle about a quarter of
the orange/sherry mix evenly over the sponge.

Heat the raspberry jam in the microwave for
20 seconds, or until it forms a spreadable paste.
Using a pastry brush, brush a layer of raspberry
jam on to the sherry-soaked sponge.

Pour half the custard over the jam, spreading
evenly with a spatula. Place another layer of
sponge on top, then sprinkle a third of the
remaining orange/sherry mix evenly over the
sponge. Brush a layer of raspberry jam over the
soaked sponge.

Arrange the caramelised peaches on top of the
sponge, in a neat pattern. Pour a thick layer of
cream (half the amount you have whipped) on
top of the caramelised peaches and spread
evenly.

Add another layer of sponge, and sprinkle with
half of the remaining orange/sherry mix. Brush a
layer of raspberry jam on to the soaked sponge.
Sprinkle the fresh raspberries on top of the jam.
Pour the remaining custard over the fresh
raspberries.

Add the final layer of sponge and sprinkle over
the rest of the orange/sherry. Brush a layer of
raspberry jam on to the soaked sponge and
spread the remaining whipped cream on top.

Decorate the top of the trifle with the grated
chocolate. Keep refrigerated.

BANOFFEE PIE

This is one of my favourite desserts and I was so excited when we made and ate it at the bakery. To make it even richer, serve it with some vanilla ice-cream on the side.

Makes one 23cm pie, serving 12–15

BASE

180g digestive biscuits
60g unsalted butter

Crush the biscuits with a rolling pin until they resemble coarse breadcrumbs.

Melt the butter in the microwave or in a pan on the hob and pour on top of the crushed biscuits. Mix until well combined. Press into the base and sides of a 23cm pie dish (ideally with a removable base). Refrigerate until set.

FILLING

1 x 397g tin of condensed milk
50g unsalted butter
50g soft brown sugar
25g golden syrup
15ml milk

To make the filling, pour the condensed milk into a medium pan. Add the butter, brown sugar and golden syrup.

Place over a medium heat until all the butter has melted and the sugar has dissolved. Turn the heat down to low and stir continuously until the mixture is thick and golden. This will take approximately 15–20 minutes.

Once the mixture is thick and golden, stir in the milk and set aside.

ASSEMBLE

2 ripe bananas
500ml double or whipping cream
50g icing sugar
chocolate shavings, to sprinkle (approx. 60g)

Peel one of the bananas and cut on the diagonal into 5mm slices. Remove the pie base from the fridge and lay the slices of banana over the base.

Pour the cooked caramel over the banana slices and spread evenly. Place in the fridge for at least 1 hour or until it has cooled and set.

Once set, peel the other banana, cut into 5mm slices and arrange on top of the set caramel.

Whip the cream and icing sugar together until they form soft/medium peaks. Cover the top of the pie with the whipped cream and sprinkle with the chocolate shavings.

CHOCOLATE PEANUT BUTTER PIE ✳

Who can resist the combination of chocolate, Oreos and peanut butter, especially if turned into a pie? You need to allow a bit of time to make this, as the various layers need time to set.

Makes one 23cm pie, serving 12–15

BASE

300g Oreo cookies
115g unsalted butter

To make the base, crush the Oreo cookies in a bag with a rolling pin until they resemble coarse breadcrumbs. Melt the butter in the microwave or in a pan on the hob, and pour on top of the cookies. Mix until well combined. Press into a 23cm tin and refrigerate until set. This should take about 30–60 minutes.

CHOCOLATE FILLING

175g dark chocolate (70% cocoa solids)
75g milk chocolate
250ml double cream
20g unsalted butter, melted

To make the chocolate filling, put the chocolate into a heatproof bowl and set aside.

Heat the cream in the microwave or in a pan on the hob until it just starts to boil, then remove from the heat and pour directly over the chocolate. Stir with a spatula until the chocolate has melted and is well combined. Let it cool for about 5 minutes. Stir in the melted butter.

Remove the pie base from the fridge and pour the chocolate mixture evenly over it. Refrigerate for at least 4 hours, until set.

TOPPING

150g cream cheese, at room temperature
160g smooth peanut butter
200g icing sugar, sifted
200ml double or whipping cream

To make the topping, put the cream cheese, peanut butter and icing sugar into a bowl. Beat with an electric mixer until smooth and lump-free, then set aside.

In a separate bowl, beat the cream until it forms soft peaks. Take a third of the cream and fold it into the peanut butter mixture with a spatula, then fold in the remaining cream. Be careful not to overmix.

ASSEMBLE

Spread the peanut butter cream evenly on top of the pie and serve.

CHOCOLATE MARSHMALLOW PIE

A variation on the pie on the preceding page, this alternative is equally tasty and rich and would look very pretty on a Christmas table with the marshmallow icing piled high.

Makes one 23cm pie, serving 12–15

BASE

300g Oreo cookies
115g unsalted butter

Crush the Oreo cookies in a bag with a rolling pin until they resemble coarse breadcrumbs.
  Melt the butter in the microwave or in a small pan on the hob, and pour on top of the cookies. Mix until well combined. Press into a 23cm pie tin and refrigerate until set. This should take about 30–60 minutes.

FILLING

1 batch of chocolate filling (see Chocolate Peanut Butter Pie, page 184)

When the pie base is set, pour the filling over it and spread it out evenly. Put it back into the fridge to set for at least 4 hours.

MARSHMALLOW TOPPING

1 batch of marshmallow icing (see page 64)

ASSEMBLE

a handful of Oreo Cookies, crushed

To assemble, spread the marshmallow icing evenly on top of the set chocolate pie and sprinkle with crushed Oreo cookies.
  Any uneaten pie will keep in the fridge for a couple of days.

MINT AND WHITE CHOCOLATE PIE

The freshness of the mint and the sweetness of the white chocolate make a great combination and a very seasonally coloured pie.

Makes one 20cm pie, serving 10–12

BASE

200g Oreo cookies
70g unsalted butter, melted

To make the base, crush the Oreos with a rolling pin or in a food processor until they resemble fine crumbs. Pour in the melted butter and pulse until the cookie crumbs are evenly coated, then press evenly into an 20cm pie tin. Refrigerate for about an hour, until set.

FILLING

315ml double cream
a handful of fresh mint leaves (approx. 10g)
170g white chocolate, chopped
2 large egg yolks
1½ tablespoons golden caster sugar
1 teaspoon peppermint extract
a few drops of green food colouring

For the filling, bring 65ml of the cream to a simmer in a pan and add the fresh mint leaves. Remove from the heat and leave to infuse for at least 10 minutes.

Put the white chocolate into a large bowl and set aside.

Put the egg yolks and sugar into a small bowl and beat until pale in colour.

Bring the cream back to a simmer and strain it into the yolk and sugar mixture, squeezing out any excess liquid from the mint leaves as you strain. Stir the mixture while adding the hot liquid. Pour the creamy mixture back into the pan and, on a low heat, stir with a wooden spoon until it thickens and coats the back of the spoon.

Strain this hot mixture on to the white chocolate and stir until completely smooth. Set aside to cool slightly.

In a separate bowl, whip the remaining cream almost to stiff peaks. Fold half the whipped cream into the white chocolate mix to lighten, then fold in the remaining whipped cream. Add the peppermint extract and a couple of drops of green food colouring.

ASSEMBLE

a handful of white chocolate shavings, to decorate

Pour the filling evenly on to the chilled base and refrigerate until firm, preferably overnight. Sprinkle the white chocolate shavings on top just before serving.

DARK CHOCOLATE AND
FRESH MINT TRUFFLE TART

Like the pie on the previous page, the chocolate and mint flavours work very well together and this tart would make the most amazing dessert. It is best to start making it two days before you plan to serve it.

Makes one 20cm pie, serving 10–12

FRESH MINT CREAM

600ml double cream
100g fresh mint leaves

First make the fresh mint cream. In a pan, bring the cream to the boil. Once it starts to boil, add the fresh mint leaves, stir and pour into a bowl. Place a piece of cling film directly on the top of the cream to prevent a skin from forming. Once it has cooled, put it into the fridge and leave to infuse overnight. Strain the cream before using, squeezing out any excess from the mint leaves.

BASE

300g Oreo cookies
100g unsalted butter, melted
2 teaspoons peppermint extract

To make the base, crush the Oreos in a bowl with a rolling pin until they resemble coarse crumbs. Pour in the melted butter and peppermint extract and mix until all the crumbs are coated. Press the mixture into a 20cm pie tin and put into the fridge for at least 1 hour to set.

FILLING

250g dark chocolate (70% cocoa solids), chopped
80g milk chocolate, chopped
215ml fresh mint cream (see opposite)
2 teaspoons peppermint extract
20g unsalted butter, at room temperature

To make the filling, put the chocolates into a heatproof bowl and set aside.

Heat the 215ml of the mint cream in the micro-wave or on the hob until it just starts to boil. Remove from the heat and pour directly over the chocolate. Add the peppermint extract and stir with a spatula until all the chocolate has melted and is well combined.

Leave to cool for about 5–10 minutes, then stir in the butter until it has all melted and is well combined.

Remove the pie base from the fridge and pour the chocolate filling over it, spreading it out evenly. Refrigerate until set, preferably overnight.

ASSEMBLE

Whip the remaining mint cream until it forms medium/stiff peaks. Serve each slice of the mint truffle tart with a scoop of mint cream on top.

Any uneaten pie will keep in the fridge for a day or two.

BOSTON CREAM PIE

A Boston cream pie is in fact a cake, not a pie, but is probably best served as a dessert – the layers of custard, chocolate and Cointreau make for a rich, creamy dinnertime treat. We owe its inclusion here to our long-standing chef Mary, whom it is always such a pleasure to see in the bakery kitchens at the weekends when she works.

Makes one 20cm layer cake, serving 10–12

VANILLA CREAM

180ml milk
375ml double cream
zest of 1 orange
3 large egg yolks
115g granulated sugar
2 tablespoons cornflour
a few teaspoons of orange liqueur, such as
  Cointreau (optional)

To make the vanilla cream, bring the milk and 250ml of the cream to a simmer in a pan, then add the orange zest. Leave to infuse for 10 minutes.

In a bowl, whisk together the yolks, sugar and cornflour until smooth. Bring the cream back to a simmer and then strain over the yolk mixture, whisking to combine.

Pour the mixture back into the pan on a low heat, stirring constantly until it comes to a boil and is thick. The mixture must be stirred constantly to prevent it from sticking and burning on the bottom of the pan. Pour it into a bowl,

place a layer of cling film directly on top of the mixture, to prevent a skin from forming, and leave to cool. Once cool, refrigerate until set.

Once set, whip the remaining 125ml of cream until medium/stiff peaks form and fold into the pastry cream with a spatula. If desired, fold in a few teaspoons of orange liqueur, to taste.

Cover with cling film and keep refrigerated until ready to use.

CAKE

210g plain flour
1½ teaspoons baking powder
½ teaspoon salt
3 large eggs, at room temperature, separated
340g granulated sugar
180ml milk
1 teaspoon vanilla extract
1 tablespoon unsalted butter, melted
orange liqueur, to soak the cake

To make the cake, preheat the oven to 180°C/160°C (fan)/gas mark 4. Grease two 20cm sandwich tins and line with parchment paper.

Sift the flour, baking powder and salt into a bowl and set aside.

In another bowl, using an electric mixer, beat the egg yolks with half the sugar until pale and fluffy and resembling ribbons when you lift the mixer. Gently fold in the milk, vanilla and melted butter until smooth. Fold in the flour mixture with a spatula.

In a clean bowl, beat the egg whites with the remaining sugar until shiny and forming stiff peaks. Fold them gently into the yolk/sugar mix, being careful not to knock too much air out.

Divide the mixture between the 2 cake tins and spread out evenly. Bake in the oven for 20–25 minutes, until golden brown and an inserted skewer comes out clean. Allow to cool in their tins for 10 minutes, then turn out on to a wire rack to cool completely.

Once cool, brush the surfaces lightly with orange liqueur.

GLAZE

130g dark chocolate (70% cocoa solids), chopped or broken into pieces
140ml double cream
1 tablespoon unsalted butter
80g golden syrup
2 tablespoons orange liqueur

To make the glaze, put the chocolate into a bowl and set aside. Heat the cream, butter and syrup in a pan until just starting to simmer. Pour this over the dark chocolate and let it sit for 3–5 minutes, then stir to combine and melt the chocolate. Stir in the orange liqueur, and refrigerate until it reaches a spreading consistency.

ASSEMBLE

To assemble the pie, place one of the cakes on a board or cake plate. Spread 2 large dollops of the vanilla cream in the centre and spread evenly. Place the second cake over the vanilla cream. Spread and swirl the glaze all over the top of the cake.

FREE FROM

When the bakery started ten years ago, it was hard to imagine that the demand for cakes that were gluten-, dairy- or sugar-free would become so high. Today we have gluten-free cupcakes and quite often a cake available every day for sale, and we are continually working on new 'free from' recipes.

Christmas should not be a time when those wishing to continue to enjoy any of these cakes should be forgotten, so a whole chapter of them seemed to fit in perfectly. Of course, they can be made and eaten throughout the year.

GLUTEN-FREE VANILLA CUPCAKES

We think these cupcakes taste as good as our normal vanilla cupcakes but are a great option for those on a gluten-free diet. They won't last quite as long, but will have a lower GI than the regular cupcakes, which also makes them better for diabetics (minus the icing though!).

Makes 12 regular cupcakes

200g unsalted butter, at room temperature
180g golden caster sugar
2 large eggs
1 teaspoon vanilla extract
150g brown rice flour
2 teaspoons gluten-free baking powder
a pinch of salt
3 tablespoons semi-skimmed milk

Preheat the oven to 180°C/160°C (fan)/gas mark 4. Line a 12-hole muffin tin with 12 muffin cases.

Cream the butter and sugar until light and fluffy. Add the eggs one at a time, ensuring the first one is well combined before adding the next. Add the vanilla and mix until combined.

Sift in the flour, baking powder and salt and mix until well combined. Pour in the milk and beat until smooth.

Spoon the mixture into the muffin cases and bake for 15–18 minutes, until golden brown or until an inserted skewer comes out clean. Allow the cupcakes to cool in the tin for about 10 minutes, then place on a wire rack to cool completely.

VANILLA BUTTERCREAM ICING

110g unsalted butter
4 tablespoons semi-skimmed milk
1 teaspoon vanilla extract
500g icing sugar
food colouring (optional)
sprinkles or other decorations

Put the butter, milk, vanilla extract and half the icing sugar in a bowl and, using an electric hand mixer, beat on a low speed until well combined. Add the remaining icing sugar and mix until smooth. Increase the speed to medium and mix for a further 30 seconds.

If you want to colour the icing, add a few drops of your chosen colouring and beat again to reach the shade you want. Ice the cupcakes and decorate as desired.

QUINOA CUPCAKES

Quinoa has been recognised as a supergrain – it is high in protein, gluten-free and easy to digest, and works fantastically well in these cupcakes. It gives them a slightly nutty texture, and with the chocolate glaze makes a cupcake that is gluten-free, dairy-free and free from refined sugar.

Makes 14 regular cupcakes

130g quinoa
320ml water
4 large eggs
80ml almond milk
1 teaspoon vanilla extract
100g vegetable oil
320g agave nectar
80g cocoa powder
1½ teaspoons baking powder
½ teaspoon salt
½ teaspoon bicarbonate of soda

Put the quinoa and the water into a pan and place on the hob over a medium/high heat. Bring to the boil, then turn the heat down to a simmer. Cover and simmer for 10 minutes, or until the water has been absorbed. Turn off the heat and allow to cool, covered.

Preheat the oven to 180°C/160°C (fan)/ gas mark 4. Line two 12-hole muffin tins with 14 muffin cases.

Put the eggs, almond milk and vanilla into a food processor and blend for 2 minutes. Add the cooked quinoa and the oil and blend for 4 minutes. Add the rest of the ingredients and blend for a further 2 minutes.

Divide the mixture between the muffin cases and bake for 20–25 minutes, or until an inserted skewer comes out clean. Allow to cool in the tins for about 10 minutes, then place on a wire rack to cool completely.

Note: The cakes will be quite soft to touch when cooked. Be careful not to overbake, as this will dry out the sponge.

FOR THE AGAVE GLAZE

155g cocoa powder
125g agave nectar
200–230ml cold water

To make the agave glaze, put the cocoa powder, agave nectar and 200ml of water into a bowl. Mix with a spatula or hand-held mixer until it is smooth. It should be spreadable and not pull away from the cake when used. It should not be so thin that it runs off the cake either. Add more water if needed.

Ice the cupcakes with the glaze and serve.

CHOCOLATE VEGAN LAYER CAKE

This cake is free from all animal products, which also makes it dairy-free. However, I am sure anyone would enjoy it, whether they follow a vegan diet or not.

Makes one 20cm layer cake

250g plain flour
75g cocoa powder
360g golden caster sugar
2½ teaspoons instant coffee powder
2½ teaspoons bicarbonate of soda
¼ teaspoon salt
310ml warm water
112ml vegetable oil
1¼ teaspoons vanilla extract
1¼ teaspoons apple cider vinegar

Preheat the oven to 180°C/160°C (fan)/gas mark 4. Grease two 20cm sandwich tins and line with parchment paper.

Place all the dry ingredients in a bowl and make a well in the centre. In a separate bowl combine all the wet ingredients. Pour the wet ingredients into the dry ingredients, then, using an electric mixer, beat on a low speed until everything is thoroughly combined.

Divide the batter evenly between the sandwich tins and bake for 30–35 minutes, or until an inserted skewer comes out clean. Allow the cakes to cool in their tins for 10 minutes, then place on a wire rack to cool completely. Carefully peel the parchment paper from the base of the cakes.

CHOCOLATE GLAZE

30g cocoa powder
300g icing sugar, sifted
4 tablespoons water

Combine all the chocolate glaze ingredients in a bowl and beat on a low speed until thoroughly combined.

ASSEMBLE

Put one of the sponges on a board or plate and cover with some of the glaze. Place the other sponge on top and use the remaining glaze to ice the top of the cake. It will be slightly runny glaze, so it will be slightly harder to use – be patient. Allow to set a little before serving.

HONEY AND ALMOND GLUTEN-FREE CAKE

A great gluten-free option and a lovely combination of flavours. This would be nice served either warm or when fully cooled.

Makes one 20cm cake, serving 10–12

4 large eggs, separated
50ml vegetable oil
280ml honey
1 teaspoon vanilla extract
300g ground almonds
¼ teaspoon salt
¼ teaspoon bicarbonate of soda
a handful of flaked almonds, to sprinkle

Preheat the oven to 180°C/160°C (fan)/gas mark 4. Lightly grease a deep 20cm cake tin and line it with parchment paper.

Using an electric hand mixer, in a bowl, beat the egg yolks, vegetable oil, honey and vanilla extract on a medium/high speed until pale and fluffy. Fold in the ground almonds, salt and bicarbonate of soda, using a spatula.

In a clean bowl, whisk the egg whites until they form stiff peaks. Fold the egg whites gently into the almond mixture. Pour into the prepared cake tin and spread out evenly. Sprinkle the flaked almonds around the edge.

Bake on the middle rack of the oven for 45–50 minutes, until golden brown or an inserted skewer comes out clean. It will brown quickly, so cover with a piece of foil while baking. Allow to cool in the tin for 10 minutes, then turn out and either leave to cool completely or serve while still warm.

SPICED HONEY LOAF

This moist, gluten-free loaf would be good served at any time of day and keeps well in an airtight container to snack on whenever you feel like it. It doesn't actually contain any honey!

Makes one 900g loaf, giving 8–10 slices

1 teaspoon bicarbonate of soda
3 tablespoons Kiddush wine (or a sweet red wine)
210g golden syrup
110ml vegetable oil
80g golden caster sugar
150g white rice flour
1 teaspoon ground mixed spice
1 teaspoon ground ginger
½ teaspoon ground cinnamon
½ teaspoon gluten-free baking powder
2 large eggs
200ml warm water (boiled)

Preheat the oven to 180°C/160°C (fan)/gas mark 4.

Lightly grease a loaf tin and line with parchment paper or with a loaf tin liner.

Dissolve the bicarbonate of soda in the wine in a small bowl and set aside. Pour the golden syrup and oil into a large bowl and place all the remaining dry ingredients on top. Stir to combine.

Add the eggs and the wine mixture and mix thoroughly. Pour in the water and mix until it is smooth. The batter will be quite liquid and grey in colour. Pour it into the loaf tin and place on the middle shelf of the oven. Bake for 50–60 minutes, until the cake is a dark golden brown and an inserted skewer comes out clean.

Note: This cake will brown very quickly when cooking, so if it takes on a lot of colour, cover the top towards the end of the cooking time with a piece of foil.

Allow to cool in the tin for about 10 minutes, then turn out on to a wire rack to cool completely.

EDIBLE GIFTS

Probably one of the nicest presents anyone could receive is an edible one — so we have put together a chapter of perfect gift ideas for Christmas and beyond, even including some for dogs, who, as any Primrose Bakery lover knows, are very important to us and mustn't be left out.

A great way of packaging edible gifts is in the increasingly popular Kilner jars that are now much easier to get hold of. They keep everything airtight but also look so nice, especially tied with a ribbon to finish off. You could also use any number of airtight boxes, bags, ribbon, paper — to make the gift as simply or elaborately wrapped as you want. Or you could simply eat any of these yourself (even the dog treats, which are entirely edible for humans).

CARAMELISED NUTS

I have to say that at the end of a working day, I look forward to a drink and some nuts and I would be delighted to receive either of these nut recipes as a gift. They would like beautiful packaged in some clear jars, tied with a ribbon at the rim.

200g soft brown sugar
4 tablespoons golden syrup or
  light corn syrup
60g unsalted butter
3 teaspoons ground cinnamon
¼ teaspoon ground nutmeg
¼ teaspoon ground cloves
100ml water
600g mixed raw nuts (such as pecans,
  almonds, walnuts)

Preheat the oven to 150°C/130°C (fan)/gas mark 2.

Put all the nuts on a lined baking tray and spread them out. Set aside.

Combine all the remaining ingredients in a pan and bring to the boil on the hob. Simmer, stirring continuously, on a low/medium heat for 2–3 minutes or until the mixture becomes syrup-like.

Pour the syrup over the nuts and stir to coat.

Put the tray of nuts into the oven and bake for approximately 30–40 minutes, stirring every 10 minutes.

Remove the nuts from the oven and allow to cool completely before packaging. They should keep well in an airtight container for a week or two.

SAVOURY NUT MIX

The only savoury recipe in this very sweet-orientated recipe book, this deserves its place here, to join the caramelised nuts recipe as another easy-to-make but delicious and pretty edible gift.

3 tablespoons olive or nut oil
1 tablespoon honey
1 clove garlic, crushed
2 tablespoons smoked paprika
1 tablespoon sweet paprika
2 teaspoons cumin seeds
¼ teaspoon ground coriander
¼ teaspoon chilli powder (optional)
1½ teaspoons sea salt (optional), plus extra
  for sprinkling
500g mixed nuts (such as walnuts, pecans,
  cashews, almonds and Brazil nuts)

Preheat the oven to 180°C/160°C (fan)/gas mark 4. Lightly grease a baking tray and line with parchment paper.

In a frying pan over a low heat, combine the oil, honey, garlic, spices and salt and cook, stirring constantly. Once well combined and fragrant (being careful not to burn the spices), add the nuts to the pan and stir to coat.

Cook on a medium/low heat for a couple of minutes, making sure the nuts are well coated with the spice mixture. Transfer the nuts to the prepared baking tray and spread them out evenly to ensure an even bake. Bake for 20–25 minutes, or until the nuts are golden brown, stirring occasionally.

Serve warm, sprinkled with extra sea salt, if you wish. Once cool, they can be stored in a clean airtight container for up to 2 weeks.

SWEET AND SALTY POPCORN

Popcorn has (rightly) got extremely popular in the last few years, so we thought we should include our own recipe here, as it is so easy to make it at home.

2 tablespoons vegetable oil
85g popping corn
15g golden caster sugar
fleur de sel, for sprinkling

Place the oil and popping corn in a medium/ large pan and swirl to coat the corn.

Sprinkle the sugar evenly over the top, shaking the pan lightly to ensure the corn is all coated. Cover the pan with a lid and place it on the hob over a medium heat. Once the kernels start popping, turn the heat down to low and regularly shake the pan gently to ensure it doesn't burn on the bottom.

Once the popping slows down significantly (about 3 or 4 pops every 8–10 seconds), take the pan off the heat, remove the lid and pour the contents into a large bowl.

To serve, sprinkle with some fleur de sel, to taste, and gently toss to coat.

MINT COCONUT ICE

Coconut ice is something that reminds us of our childhood. It is probably more often a summer's day treat, but this mint flavoured one with its pink and white colours would look pretty packaged up and given as a gift at Christmas.

Makes one 20cm square tin or 64 pieces

260g desiccated coconut
120g icing sugar, sifted
1 x 397g tin of condensed milk
3 teaspoons peppermint extract
a few drops of pink food colouring

In a large bowl, mix together the coconut and sifted icing sugar. Add the condensed milk and peppermint extract and mix with a wooden spoon until thoroughly combined.

Put half the mixture into a separate bowl and add a few drops of pink colouring and mix until it is pale pink.

Put the uncoloured portion into a 20cm square tin (with a removeable base if possible) and press down to the edges, making sure it is evenly spread out. Place in the fridge for 10–15 minutes, then put the pink portion on top of the white and spread it out evenly. Press down the top layer gently and evenly with the flat of your hand.

Cover with cling film and place in the fridge to set for at least 4–5 hours, or preferably over-night. Cut into 2.5 x 2.5cm squares and package in clear cellophane bags, tied with a ribbon.

SALTED CARAMEL TRUFFLES

A rich creamy truffle that will be hard not to eat as you package them up, so make sure you make a few extra for yourself.

Makes 36–48 truffles

SALTED CARAMEL SAUCE

165g granulated sugar
4½ tablespoons water
190ml double cream
1½ teaspoons fleur de sel

Note: This is a very hot liquid, so please be careful when making it.

Put the sugar and water into a medium pan and place over a medium heat on the hob. Do not stir the mixture, as it will cause the sugar syrup to crystallise.

Swirl the pan occasionally and gently until all the sugar has dissolved, then turn the heat up to high and let the syrup boil.

While the sugar syrup is boiling, pour the cream into another pan and add the fleur de sel. Place the cream over a medium heat until it is warm, but do not boil.

Once the sugar syrup turns a golden colour, remove it from the heat and immediately add 1–2 tablespoons of the warm cream to the pan. Stir quickly with a wooden spoon to prevent it from sticking. Be careful when adding the cream, as it will bubble up and rise very quickly, let off a lot of hot steam and may splutter.

Add the remaining cream in small amounts, continuously stirring. Pour into a heatproof bowl and set aside while you weigh out the chocolate for the truffles.

TRUFFLES

250g milk chocolate
100g dark chocolate (70% cocoa solids)
½ teaspoon fleur de sel
350g salted caramel sauce
30g unsalted butter, melted

Break the milk and dark chocolate into small pieces and put it in a heatproof bowl with the fleur de sel.

Heat the salted caramel sauce in a pan until it starts to boil. Pour the hot caramel sauce over the chocolate pieces. Stir until all the chocolate has melted and is well combined.

Leave to cool for about 5 minutes, then add the melted butter and stir until combined.

Put the bowl into the fridge until the mixture has set. This will take 6–8 hours.

ASSEMBLE

Cocoa powder, to dust

Once set, spoon out 15–20g portions of the mixture, roll into balls and then roll each truffle in cocoa powder.

You might want to package these truffles in a box, as the cocoa has a tendency to rub off if it touches against things. They are probably best made, given and eaten within a fairly short timeframe, and should be kept refrigerated if not eaten immediately.

CHRISTMAS PUDDING RUM BALLS

The Primrose Bakery version of a Christmas pudding, these tiny chocolates would be nice served after dinner with coffee and would look pretty displayed on a plate in a group.

Makes 12–18 balls (depending upon their size)

**200g dark chocolate (70% cocoa solids),
  broken into small pieces**
175ml double cream
5 tablespoons rum
**cocoa, finely crushed nuts, or sprinkles,
  to finish**
**sugar holly decorations or real holly,
  to decorate**

Cover a baking tray tightly with two layers of cling film.

Tip the chocolate into a bowl. Put the cream in a pan and bring to the boil, but only just, then pour over the chocolate and stir until it has melted. Add the rum (or other flavouring if using) and mix it in. Allow the mixture to cool at room temperature until set.

Using a melon baller or teaspoon, divide the mixture into 12 portions. Dust your hands with icing sugar to stop the mixture sticking and roll the pieces into balls. Roll them in the sifted cocoa, crushed nuts or sprinkles and place them on the prepared tray. Decorate the rum balls with holly sugar decorations, or real holly, if you wish.

To make a non-alcoholic version, the rum can be substituted with 1–2 teaspoons of vanilla, peppermint, coconut or orange extract. If you do this, make sure you increase the amount of double cream to make up for the liquid you have lost by not using the rum.

Package these carefully, so as not to allow them to touch each other or anything else too much, and eat soon after preparing and giving. Store any uneaten rum balls in the fridge.

PEANUT BUTTER AND BANANA DOG CUPCAKES

As such a dog-friendly bakery, we couldn't really leave our favourite pets out at Christmas time! So here are their own cupcakes and cake (overleaf) so they can celebrate too. These will keep and freeze well, so you can make a large batch in advance and take them round to a few special dogs.

Makes 20 mini cupcakes

1 egg
2 tablespoons honey
1 ripe banana, mashed
80g smooth peanut butter
40g wholemeal flour
45g rolled oats
½ teaspoon baking powder
70ml water

Preheat the oven to 180°C/160°C (fan)/gas mark 4. Line a mini cupcake/muffin tin with paper cases.

Put the egg, honey and mashed banana into a bowl and stir to combine. Add the peanut butter and beat together to form a smooth paste. Add the flour, oats and baking powder and stir to form a dough-like consistency. Add the water and mix until well combined.

Let this mixture sit for 15 minutes. Stir a few times, then spoon it into the paper cases, filling each about two-thirds full.

Bake for 12–15 minutes until golden brown or an inserted skewer comes out clean. Cool on a wire rack.

Store in an airtight container for 2–3 days at room temperature, or freeze so that the cupcakes can be enjoyed at another time.

DOG CHRISTMAS CAKE

We think that even a dog needs a cake to help celebrate Christmas, and our dog testers, Jack and Alfie, quickly finished this off.

Makes one 15cm cake, to serve 8 dogs

1 large egg
2 tablespoons honey
100g grated carrot
**40g apple sauce (ready-made, or
    purée some apples)**
150g wholemeal flour
½ teaspoon ground cinnamon
2 teaspoons baking powder

Preheat the oven to 180°C/160°C (fan)/gas mark 4. Lightly grease a 15cm cake tin and line with parchment paper.

Put the egg, honey, grated carrot and apple sauce into a bowl and beat until well mixed. Add the flour, cinnamon and baking powder and beat again until well combined.

Pour the batter into the cake tin and place on the middle rack of the oven. Bake for 25–30 minutes, until light golden brown and an inserted skewer comes out clean. Allow the cake to cool in its tin, then turn out on to a wire rack to cool completely before serving.

Any uneaten cake will keep, wrapped in cling film or in an airtight container, for a good few days.

MERINGUES

These are a great year-round dessert, and here we have suggested some more seasonal variations if you want to give them a go – although a plate of simple plain meringues with a bowl of whipped cream on the side is pretty amazing!

Makes 8 large or approx. 24 mini meringues

BASIC MERINGUE RECIPE

6 large egg whites
175g golden caster sugar
175g icing sugar, sifted

Preheat the oven to 120°C/100°C (fan)/gas mark ½.

Using an electric mixer, whisk the egg whites in a bowl on a low speed until the whites reach a foamy consistency. Increase the speed slightly and add the caster sugar a tablespoon at a time, allowing a few seconds between additions to ensure that it is thoroughly mixed in.

When the egg whites form stiff peaks, add the icing sugar one tablespoon at a time, again increasing the speed of the mixer until it is all added and you have a stiff, glossy meringue. This process can take a few minutes, but it is well worth it.

If making plain meringues, simply pipe or spoon the mixture on to lined baking trays and bake in the oven until they are completely dried out. If they start to brown, your oven temperature is too high, so turn it down a little. Depending on the size of your meringues, they can take from 45 minutes to 3 hours to cook. The best way to test meringues is as follows: if they have a hard enough shell that you can pick them up and you can tap them on the bottom without them breaking easily, they are done. The insides will be gooey and chewy when eaten soon after baking.

DIFFERENT FLAVOUR COMBINATIONS

Once you have made the basic meringue recipe, there are lots of ways you can flavour them to make it more interesting.

Black Forest meringues – Using the plain cooked meringues, make a small hole in the top of each one and pipe in 2–3 teaspoons of black cherry pie filling (you can buy cans of this in the supermarket). Melt a bar of dark chocolate (70% cocoa solids) and spoon some over the top of each meringue to seal in the filling. Lightly drizzle more melted chocolate over all the meringues then sprinkle with some chocolate shavings before putting them into the freezer to set.

Candy cane meringues (peppermint) – Put a few drops of liquid red food colouring into a small container and mix with peppermint flavouring until the required taste is achieved. Using a spoon, gently swirl the flavoured colouring into your meringue mixture, making sure not to overmix it, as you want to see the red swirling through the white meringue when it is baked. Pipe or spoon the meringue mixture on to lined baking trays and bake as described opposite.

Chocolate orange meringues – Simply grate the zest of an orange into the meringue mixture, then, using a spoon, swirl through some cocoa powder until evenly distributed but not completely mixed in. Pipe or spoon the meringue mixture on to lined baking trays and bake as described opposite.

Coffee and walnut meringues – Swirl some finely ground instant espresso powder through your meringue mixture, then pipe or spoon the meringue mixture on to lined baking trays and sprinkle with finely-chopped walnuts. Bake as described opposite.

TUTTI FRUTTI NOUGAT

This would make a lovely gift – it's little bit tricky to make but the end result is delicious, and it can be made in advance. This might be the time to invest in a candy thermometer, as it really does help with getting the marshmallow and sugar temperatures right and is straightforward to use.

Makes about 14 pieces (depending upon their size)

MARSHMALLOW BASE

250ml water
75g golden syrup
205g white granulated sugar
2 egg whites

The marshmallow base is best made using a candy thermometer if you have one. Put the water, golden syrup and caster sugar in a pan. Clip the candy thermometer to the inside of the pan and heat the mixture to 117°C over a medium heat. If you don't have a thermometer, this should take about 5 minutes and small bubbles start to form.

  Meanwhile, in a large bowl whisk the egg whites to stiff peaks. Once the syrup reaches the required temperature, slowly pour it in a steady stream into the egg whites and beat until thick and glossy on a medium/high speed. This should take about 2–3 minutes. Set aside.

NOUGAT

4 tablespoons water
450g light corn syrup
615g white granulated sugar
60g butter, melted
1 teaspoon vanilla extract
250g dried fruit (such as cranberries, cherries, blueberries, apricots), roughly chopped
250g nuts (such as pistachios, almonds, hazelnuts), toasted and roughly chopped

Line the base of a 36 x 25cm baking tin with a sheet of edible rice paper.

  Put the water, syrup and sugar in a pan and bring to the boil over a medium heat. Using your thermometer, boil until the temperature reaches 137°C.

  Meanwhile, put the marshmallow base in a stand mixer. Once the syrup reaches 137°C, slowly add it to the marshmallow in a steady stream, beating on a low speed.

  Pour in the melted butter and vanilla and mix until combined. Finally fold in the roughly chopped dried fruit and the nuts and mix until combined.

  Pour the mixture into the prepared tin and cover with another sheet of rice paper. Smooth out with a rolling pin and weight down overnight with a heavy chopping board.

  Cut the nougat to your desired shape and size and store in an airtight container.

POPCORN BAUBLES

These crazy baubles are fun to make and eat and children will love to get involved. They probably won't last long hanging on the tree without someone being tempted to take them down and eat them.

Makes 12 baubles

POPCORN

2 tablespoons vegetable oil
100g popping corn

Put the oil and popping corn into a large pan. Swirl the pan around to coat all the kernels with oil.

Cover and put the pan on the hob over a medium heat. Once the kernels start to pop, turn the heat down to low and regularly shake the pan gently to ensure it doesn't burn on the bottom.

Once the popping slows down significantly (about 3 or 4 pops every 8–10 seconds), take the pan off the heat, remove the lid and pour the contents into a large bowl. Allow to cool completely.

BAUBLES

12 wrapped chocolates (e.g. Lindor chocolate balls)
12 pieces of ribbon (35cm in length)
90g salted butter
350g fluffy marshmallows
100g popcorn

To make the baubles, tie one end of each ribbon on to one end of each chocolate ball wrapper. Tie the other end of the ribbon on to the same end of the sweet wrapper to make a loop, making sure it is tied securely. Place the chocolates in the fridge while you prepare the popcorn.

Line a baking tray with parchment paper and set aside. Put the butter into a suitable bowl and melt in the microwave (or melt it in a pan over the hob). Once melted, add the marshmallows and microwave again in 20-second bursts (or heat them in the pan) until the marshmallows are soft and liquid. Add the popcorn and fold through until all combined. Allow the mixture to cool slightly before you begin moulding.

To prevent the mixture from sticking to your hands, dip your hands in cold water. Place a small handful of popcorn mixture in the palm of your hand and flatten it out. Place one of the cold chocolate balls on the popcorn, with the ribbon facing up. Wrap the popcorn mixture around the chocolate ball, adding more to create a bauble, pressing the popcorn mixture tightly round the chocolate by cupping between both hands. Once the wrapped chocolate is completely covered, place on the baking tray, ribbon facing upwards. Continue until all the chocolates are covered. Place in the fridge overnight or until set, then hang the baubles on the Christmas tree.

GINGERBREAD HOUSE

Our chef Daniel made a replica of the bakery in gingerbread for our Christmas window display and it was a huge success, so we thought we should encourage others to make a gingerbread house for themselves – it is also a fun way to pass a cold, grey afternoon and looks impressive when you have finished.

Makes one 15 x 15cm house, with a little left over for gingerbread men

You will need a 20cm cake board to sit the house on.

GINGERBREAD

150g dark brown sugar
100g golden syrup
50g black treacle
zest of 1 orange
2 teaspoons ground cinnamon
2 teaspoons ground ginger
a pinch of ground cloves
2 tablespoons water
190g unsalted butter
450g plain flour

Put the sugar, golden syrup, black treacle, orange zest and spices in a pan and heat until all of the sugar has dissolved. Stir in the butter and water until well combined.

Sift the flour into a bowl. Add the liquid mixture to the flour and combine until a soft dough is formed. Wrap the dough in cling film and put into the fridge to chill for at least an hour before using.

TEMPLATE

Take 2 sheets of A4 paper and cut out the following shapes:

Side walls: 15 x 15cm square
Roof panels: 18 x 12.5cm rectangle
Front/back panel: 15 x 23cm rectangle, folding down the top 2 corners to meet in the middle and create a central point

TO PREPARE THE HOUSE

Preheat the oven to 180°C/160°C (fan)/gas mark 4.

Divide the gingerbread dough into 6 equal portions. Roll each piece out on a sheet of baking parchment to 7mm thick. Using the templates as a guide, cut out the sections for the roof, sides, front and back of the house – any left-over trimmings can be used to make gingerbread men. Transfer the gingerbread sections on their baking parchment to 3 baking trays and bake in the oven for 10–12 minutes or until just firm in the centre. If you don't have 3 baking trays, you can bake the sections in batches. If any of the edges are particularly misshapen after baking, simply trim with a sharp knife while the gingerbread is still warm. Set aside to cool completely.

ASSEMBLE

200g white chocolate
vanilla buttercream (see page 80), to decorate
sweets/chocolates, to decorate

Note: If you wish to pipe a design on the front panel of the house, this should be done before assembly and left to dry.

Melt the white chocolate either in a bowl over a pan of simmering water on the hob or carefully in a microwave. Transfer the melted chocolate to a piping bag fitted with a small round nozzle.
  Pipe some chocolate along the bottom edge of the back panel and hold in place on the cake board. Pipe some chocolate along the bottom and one side edge of one of the side panels and place on the board, attaching it to the back panel. Hold these pieces in place until the chocolate has set and the walls can support themselves. Repeat this step with the remaining side wall, attaching it to the back panel and cake board, and leave to set.
  Once the structure is stable, pipe along both exposed side edges of the side walls and the bottom edge of the front panel and join them all together. Hold in place until set.
  Pipe along the diagonal exposed edges of the front and back panels. Attach the roof panels and hold until set. Fill the central gap between the roof panels with melted chocolate.
  Once all of the chocolate has set and you have a sturdy structure, you are ready to decorate your gingerbread house in whatever way you like. To pipe a roof detail onto your house, place some vanilla buttercream in a piping bag and pipe a pattern directly onto the roof. The buttercream can also be used to attach sweets and sugar decorations to your house.

CARAMEL APPLES

These would be fun to make on a cold winter's afternoon, then eaten for tea or with friends or wrapped individually and given as gifts.

Makes 18

455g dark brown sugar
225g unsalted butter, at room temperature
1 x 397g tin of sweetened condensed milk
225g golden syrup
115g maple syrup
½ teaspoon vanilla extract
1 teaspoon (dark) molasses or black treacle
¼ teaspoon salt
18 medium apples
assorted decorations (such as chopped nuts, chopped raisins, mini M&Ms and sugar sprinkles)

You will need a candy thermometer for this recipe, and 18 sturdy lollipop sticks or chopsticks.

Combine the sugar, butter, condensed milk, corn syrup, maple syrup, vanilla, molasses and salt in a large, heavy-based pan. Stir with a wooden spoon on a medium/low heat until all the sugar dissolves. There should be no grittiness (sugar crystals) when you test by rubbing a little of the caramel between your fingers. Brush down the sides of the pan with a wet pastry brush to dissolve any sugar crystals that might form.
    Attach the candy thermometer to the inside of the pan and cook the caramel at a rolling boil until the temperature reaches 113°C, stirring constantly and slowly with a spatula. Continue to occasionally brush the sides down with the pastry brush. Carefully pour the caramel into a metal bowl and leave to cool to 93°C, at which point you are ready to dip the apples.
    While the caramel is cooling, cover a baking tray with a layer of parchment paper. Insert a chopstick or sturdy lollipop stick into each apple at the stem end, about 5cm down into the apple core.
    When the caramel has cooled enough for dipping, dip the apples in, one by one, holding by the stick and lowering the apple into the caramel, submerging all but the very top of the apple. Pull the apple up from the caramel and let the excess caramel drip off from the bottom back into the pan. Then place on the lined baking tray. The caramel will pool a little at the bottom of each apple. Put in the fridge to chill for at least 15 minutes.
    Once the caramel has chilled, remove the apples from the fridge and use your fingers to press the caramel that has dripped to the bottom back up on to the apples. Put your selected decorations in separate bowls, and holding each apple by its stick, dip it in the decorations and swirl a little to coat well. Return the decorated apples to the fridge to chill for at least 1 hour.

ACKNOWLEDGEMENTS

This is the first book on my own now Lisa has left the bakery, and one that is very important to me, and it has been a real pleasure for me to work on it alongside the dedicated Primrose Bakery staff.

Our inspiring former chef, Lisa Chan, has been invaluable in recipe development, organisation, enthusiasm and a genuine talent to work alongside and I cannot thank her enough for her hard work and loyalty. From London to Hong Kong and back to her native Australia, she has worked tirelessly to help me create something very special.

The bakery's former business manager, Faye MacGregor, has been a true friend to me and an enormous asset to the bakery and to the book, as have Sally Humphreys and Rachel Wicking, and all three of them have my huge thanks and appreciation. The bakery's newest head chef, Daniel Harding, has already made a huge impression at the bakery and has an enormous talent, and it has been great to have him involved so much in this book with recipes and styling.

The rest of the staff are equally important to me, to the bakery and to the books – working for a small business is often hard and unrewarding, but the general work ethic and sense of fun and talent they bring has got the bakery to where it is today and beyond, and I can honestly say it is a pleasure to go to work every day.

My two daughters, Daisy and Millie, deserve special thanks – I am sure having a mother who has quite often put cakes and work before them in the last ten years has been very difficult and frustrating for them at times, but they have developed into intelligent, hard-working girls whom I am enormously proud of, especially in the light of some of the ups and downs the last few years have thrown at us. The rest of my family have been instrumental in contributing to the success of the bakery and the books and I am forever grateful to them for the support they give me – my mother, Caroline, my brother Daniel and his son Leo, my father, Jeremy, and my stepmother, Camilla, and her daughters, Louise and Lizzy.

My agent, Charlotte Robertson, continues to be not only a brilliant agent but a good friend, and on this book it has been exciting to work with a new editor, Daniel Hurst, and a new photographer, Stuart Ovenden, and also again with the talented Alice Whiting and Friederike Huber. At Square Peg, Rosemary Davidson and Rowan Yapp play a vital role in commissioning and producing the bakery books. Our chefs Laurel, Becky, Manda and Mary have also helped with some delicious recipes for this book. For overall help with the business, I would like to thank Andrew Newland for his knowledge and support.

Last, but by no means least, thanks must go to Ray Winters for his many cake ideas, mostly fantastic and now firm favourites at the bakery, and a few a little far-fetched! Also for his amazing support of the bakery and invaluable help to me over the last few years. Thank you.

INDEX